THE SUPERNATURAL POWER OF
TEARS

Turning Our Hearts Back to the Father

Derrick Snodgrass, Jr.

Dedication

I would like to dedicate this book to my heavenly Father for being so faithful to me and patient with me. It has been quite a spiritual journey to learn who you are and just how much you love me. I lost my mind to darkness in the fall of humanity, but now, by your grace, I can see clearly and experience the reality of my identity in Christ.

Jesus, thank you for being my friend, my Savior, and my elder brother. I would be eternally grateful to merely wash your feet or eat the crumbs that fall from your table, but you have pulled up a chair and told me to come eat beside you. I cannot that believe you summonsed me to the king's table. Through your own glory and excellence, you have given us your precious and magnificent promises, so that through them we may become partakers of the divine nature (1 Peter 1:4).

Holy Spirit, you truly are my best friend—a constant friend. You are not a dove, a fire, or a wind. You are a person: the active, operative, presence and power of God that quickens me to carry out the Father's will. Thank you for your wisdom and your direction. You have saved me from too many shipwrecks to name.

Father, I'm blessed in you; Jesus I'm obsessed with you; and Holy Spirit, I'm possessed by you! Thank you for bringing me back to your heart!

All Scripture quotations are from the New King James Version of the Holy Bible, unless noted otherwise.

The Supernatural Power of Tears
Turning our Hearts Back to the Father
Copyright © 2021

Published By
Amazon KDP Publishing
Derrick M. Snodgrass Jr.
Glory takeover Ministries
Anderson, IN 46013

All rights reserved under International Copyright Law. This publication may not be reproduced, stored in a retrieval system, or transmitted in whole or in part, in any form or by any means, electronic, mechanical, photocopying, recording or otherwise, without prior express written permission of the publisher.

Cover design: Derrick M. Snodgrass. Jr.

Printed in the United States of America

Acknowledgments

My Three Children

Jonathan, we are so glad to know that you watch over us and we find so much comfort in knowing you are in heaven with Jesus. We regret that we did not get to know you on this side, but we look forward to reuniting with you again in eternity!

Jackson, you make me such a proud father. You are one of the smartest, most articulate kids that I know. Your passion for God and your spiritual insight inspires me every day.

Khloe, I love you, my beautiful girl. You literally melt my heart. You are already sassy and full of fire. I know that you are going to be a trailblazer for the kingdom!

My Parents, Derrick and Diann Snodgrass

Thank you both for doing such a great job in raising us kids, and for being there for us anytime we needed you. I appreciate your love and support that you've offered in any way that I've needed it. You guys have been constant friends. Thanks for setting a great example of what a balanced life looks like. Mom, thanks for imparting your spiritual hunger and spiritual gifts to me. You guys have taught us that it is not about the life you live, but it's about the legacy that you leave behind. I intend to finish strong and make you guys proud. I love you both so much!

Pastor Todd Smith

  Todd, when I first came to Georgia, I was not looking for mentorship (even though I needed it). I just wanted God's presence and to know God intimately. God gave me what I wanted and needed when I met you! Your passion for God, and the fact that you are the same behind the scenes and on stage is super rare and hard to find. It has been an honor to serve with you and Pastor Karen.

  You bring a healthy balance to the supernatural that is full of word and spirit! You share my spiritual DNA. Thank you for imparting so much to me and my family. Thank you for believing in me, for always being available whenever I call, and for reaching out to me to show you care. Nobody says "BRRRROOOOO" like you! Thanks for being a great mentor, leader, and friend! I know you have lived your whole life for the moment that you are in right now. You are truly an inspiration to the whole world!

Pastor Doss

Thank you so much for covering me and my family. I appreciate everything that you have done for us, and for always being there when I needed you. I do not believe that it was a coincidence the way God reconnected our families. I appreciate your prayers, love, guidance, and support. Thank you for every opportunity that you have given me. It is so awesome to find a leader I can trust and recognize that he has my best interests at heart. I appreciate all of our talks, laughs, and biblical debates. I am thankful that our pastor-sheep relationship is not a theocracy, but a democracy. You allow me to have a voice and we glean from each other.

My church family, S.P.E.C. (Spiritual Prosperity Enrichment Center)

Thank you all for your love for me and my family. We appreciate your prayers, your sacrifices, your hard work, and your dedication to the kingdom. It has been such an honor to pastor you all for five years. We love our church family.

My Wife

Thank you for everything that you have done for me. You are such an amazing person, and I am so blessed to be able to do life with you! It has been such an amazing journey, and we're just getting started. I'm so thankful for your love, support, and encouragement! It has been so awesome to see your growth and maturity over these past 8 years. The work that God has done in your life has been nothing short of miraculous. I am so godly proud of you!

I am so hungry for more of God and it would be difficult for me to pursue Him in the way that I have without your blessing. Thank you for your compassion, patience, and understanding. It is also so great to know that you are just as hungry as I am, and we bless and sharpen each other. Every sacrifice you have made for our family is appreciated. It is commendable the way you work, care for our children, do the administrative work in the ministry, and pursue your own dreams! I LOVE YOU, and I'm excited to see what else God has in store for us!

Foreword

Every few years a book crosses your path that rocks you to the core of your soul; THIS IS THAT BOOK! *The Supernatural Power of Tears: Turning our Hearts back to the Father*, will find a way of disturbing your comfort zone while challenging you to pursue the face of God unlike any other time in your life. Let me say front and center: THIS BOOK IS ABOUT REVIVAL! It's about brokenness and contrition, it is about falling back in-love with Jesus. In this hour, we no longer need authors giving us "self-help" principles that enhance and posture-up our flesh, no, we need works like this one that call us deeper,... deeper repentance, deeper faith, and deeper love. WARNING; this book will not allow us to settle into mediocrity and carnality; it will take you higher!

When my friend Derrick Snodgrass Jr., told me that God had given him a book to write I listened intently to what the Lord said to him. As Derrick spoke about the essence of the book my spirit man literally leapt inside of me. Then, as I read the pages I was moved to tears. I couldn't believe what I was reading. It was fresh bread! A fresh word from heaven! I have to admit the more I read the more my soul was lit on fire and I hungered for more of God! It didn't take long for me to realize this was a Kingdom message that had to be released to the world.

As your friend I must warn you, when you read this book it will cause things to shift in your life. Things you had no idea were even out of place. You will discover every page is dripping with love, compassion, revelation, and conviction. It is so well written that you will not want to put it down. God's voice will echo from the formed words on the page. You will hear His voice and He will beckon you to find a dark room and simply draw near to Him. It's okay to lay the book down and pursue the Father. This is the intent of Derrick Snodgrass, Jr. His whole purpose is to reveal to you the secret chambers of the Father's heart.

Very few leaders have captivated me the way Derrick has, His brokenness and humility are contagious. Being around him causes you to want to love Jesus more! He walks so gently before the Lord. I have no doubt this young man, at this crucial juncture in history, is being raised up by God to speak His heart. I have a front row seat and right before my eyes God is elevating Derrick's voice to the nation and the world. This book reveals that God has given him an authentic end-time message, a message that can change the world.

Being one with the Father and pursuing more of his presence is the greatest call on any of our lives. Everything we will ever do in the earth concerning purpose flows out of that place of intimacy and oneness with God! Many of you reading this know what God has been doing at Christ Fellowship Church through the North Georgia Revival. We have experienced an unprecedented amount of God's glory in ways that are unfathomable. Over the past two years of the revival, we have seen scars instantly vanish before our eyes, cancers eradicated, 250 tumors dissolved, blinded eyes opened, ADHD healed, hepatitis disappear, people discharged from hospice with a prognosis of just weeks to live, radical salvations, marriages restored, demons cast out, and so much more!

Yet, we are believing for even more of God's glory to engulf the revival, our church, our city, and this nation!

Before any of the healings, signs, miracles, or wonders happened, I remember crying out to God in travail. I was tired, burned out, and broken before the Lord. After pastoring for over 25 years, I was tired of mediocre, mundane Christianity. I was tired of cute church. I was tired of praise and worship with the perfect presentation (lighting, fog machines, strobe lights and the like), but no power, no demonstration. I could not reconcile the Bible to my experience of Christianity and what we are commonly seeing in most of the churches across America.

We called our church to a 21 day fast. I had determined that if something did not break in the Spirit, if I did not see an outpouring of God's presence, I was going to resign. In this period of fasting, praying, and crying out to God, I remember just being so broken before his presence. During this time our church was corporately pursuing God's presence. We never asked for any miracles. We never asked for any healings. We simply wanted to see God's face. We did not want his hand (what he could give us), we wanted His face, His presence, His person. After that period of pursuing God, I saw and experienced my first open vision: our empty baptistery was filled with water and the top was ablaze. The tank was physically empty, but in the spirit, it was full of water and ignited with fiery flames. The Holy Spirit spoke to me and said I'm going to baptize my people with Holy Spirit Fire. Today, two years and over 13,000 baptisms later, the fruit of that vision and experience has impacted the entire world and continues to do so

Jesus later spoke to me and said, "Todd, I am coming with a vengeance for my bride!" I believe the revival God wants to bring to the earth is very near; we are at the threshold of the third great awakening! I believe the world will experience the glory of God in ways that will exceed by far former moves of the Spirit, and it may not look like what we are expecting!

No move of the Spirit was ever birthed apart from prayer, not just prayer but anguish, desperation, and weeping before the Lord. I believe this book was birthed in heaven's delivery room, and Derrick was destined to write this book for such a time as this to make ready the body of Christ for what God is preparing to do in the earth. Jesus is calling His bride to true holiness, not legalism, not a dress code, not religion, but a relationship! He is recalibrating and cleansing her heart, He is removing the wrinkles from her garments, and He is starting with the house of God! The insight, the revelation, and the skill set Derrick possesses as an apologist are persuasive, convicting, and convincing! The hidden treasure of the value of our tears in heaven, and the role they play in our relationship with God and answered prayer is remarkable.

David Wilkerson said, "What is it about tears that should be so terrifying? The touch of God is marked by tears…deep, soul-shaking tears, weeping…it comes when that last barrier is down and you surrender yourself…" My question to the church is, where is the anguish? Where is true brokenness? Who will call a solemn assembly before the Lord? To see the next move of God come to pass in the earth, the church must embrace purity, sanctification, holiness, weeping, prayer, travail, and repentance. Then we will begin to see God do what only he can do in a way that only he can do it. Moses asked to see God's glory (Ex 33:18), and God responded you cannot see my face and live. Moses never asked for God's face; he asked to see His glory. I believe there is a direct correlation between the glory of God and the face of God. The more we seek His face, the more glory will be revealed in our lives. From this passage we conclude that in order to see the glory of God in our lives, our flesh MUST DIE!

Pastor Todd Smith
North Georgia Revival at Christ Fellowship Church
Author, *Speaking in Tongues, He Sat Down,* and
Creating a Habitation for God's Glory

Contents

Introduction 1

1. Why Tears? 2
2. Is God Moved by Emotion or by Faith? 8
3. Tears Are a Language That Heaven Understands ..31
4. How to Make Yourself Irresistible to God 44
5. Is It Right to Be Broken? 65
6. If It Ain't Broke, Don't Fix It! 86
7. From Brokenness to Fruitfulness 101
8. Are Tears Foolproof Access into Heaven? 120
9. The Tear Room in Heaven 129
10. Tears Will Cease 137
11. Jesus Empathizes With Your Tears 143

Conclusion 151

Bibliography 158

Introduction

Everyone has cried tears at some point in their life, and every human being was created with emotions. Some people have been taught to believe that tears are a sign of weakness, or that tears are something of which to be ashamed, or that tears are not connected to heaven moving in your favor. Biblically we will see numerous times that tears are precious to God and have great value in heaven. Literally, no tear that has ever been cried in faith, prayer, worship, victimization, or abuse has been wasted, and there is an irrefutable connection between the tears we cry and the swiftness of heaven working on our behalf. This book will provide an exciting look into God's promises pertaining to the supernatural power of tears cried out to heaven that move God to deploy angels, bring comfort to your heart, and accelerate the answers to your prayers.

1.
Why Tears?

Contrary to popular belief, tears are significant and essential functions for human beings. At one time it was thought by many that tears were pointless, and that crying was just a left over unneeded mechanism from evolution. Modern science, however, has come to a different understanding. Tears may be classified into three different categories. First, basal tears keep one's eyes constantly lubricated and are naturally occurring. Second, reflex tears are produced when the eyes get irritated by harsh aromas or physical trauma. The third kind of tears, appropriately named emotional tears, are produced when the body reacts emotionally to something.[1]

Physiologically, there are so many different ways that tears positively affect the human body. It is proven that tears have antibacterial properties (preventing blindness-causing infections), they remove toxins, they keep our eyes lubricated (aiding in comfort and clear vision), and they elevate our mood. Some of you have even heard of the term "cry it out!" When someone is angry, depressed, or anxious, crying actually helps to boost serotonin levels. Biochemist William Frey, who has been researching tears for over 15 years, found in one

---

[1] Pooja Sharma, "Why Do We Cry? The Science of Tears," *Healthy Hub* (blog), last modified July 30, 2018, https://healthyhub.org/why-do-we-cry-the-science-of-tears/.

study that emotional tears–those formed in distress or grief–contained more toxic byproducts than tears of irritation (think onion peeling).[2]

Are tears toxic then? No! They actually remove toxins from our body that build up because of stress. So there are many natural benefits of tears, but how do tears affect the spiritual realm?

> *"My only friends scoff at me; they persist in mocking me; even now my eyes well up in tears to God."*
> **—Job 16:20, *The Voice***

When asking the question "why tears?" one must understand that tears are connected to the deepest level of emotion. When someone cries, especially in the case of strong crying or weeping, there is a deep emotional connection that has been triggered and released. According to Sebastian Gendry,

> Scientists have discovered that the emotional tears contain higher levels of manganese and the hormone prolactin, which helps reduce both of these in the body, consequently this keeps depression at bay. They also contain the neurotransmitter *leucine enkephalin*, which is a natural painkiller that is released when we are stressed. Many people have found that crying

---

[2] Judith Orloff, "The Health Benefit of Tears," *Psychology Today*, last modified July 27, 2010, https://www.psychologytoday.com/us/blog/emotional-freedom/201007/the-health-benefits-tears.

actually calms them after being upset. Contrary to popular human opinion you cannot numb your emotions selectively. When you bury your sadness, you also bury your joy. If you want to feel happier, you need to accept and free your tears, because you're releasing pain. The only way to fully feel your joy is to fully feel your grief.

We need both laughter and tears to help us function as human beings. Crying relieves stress, reduces hormone and chemical levels in the body, and helps us return to a calm state. Laughter relieves stress, stimulates healing, exercises certain parts of the body, and helps in human bonding.[3]

Remember that crying is a trigger to the deepest emotional state, and that does not only mean sadness. It also means anger, grief, pain, depression, and joy. The best, most therapeutic laughs are without a doubt those gut busting laughs that bring you to full blown weeping!

Many of you reading this right now are smiling because you can remember the times you laughed so hard it brought you to tears. Just the other day, I laughed so hard with some friends that I fell out of my chair, with uncontrollable wailing and weeping. Those types of laughs carry an anointing that will cause you to walk in physical healing.

---

[3] Sebastian Gendry, "Why It Is Important to Embrace Your Tears," *Laughter Online University* (blog), accessed May 7, 2020, https://www.laughteronlineuniversity.com/importance-of-tears/.

> *"A joyful, cheerful heart brings healing to both body and soul."*
> — **Proverbs 17:22, *The Passion Translation***

This passage is often quoted as "laughter does good like a medicine." However that popular translation isn't quite accurate, since laughter won't do much for you in and of itself. When you look deeper at the Scripture, it says a "joyful heart" or a "cheerful heart," so casually laughing will not really yield the benefits of this verse. The Scripture says that the laughter or the joy has to be a constant emotion or disposition that goes beyond head knowledge; it gets into your heart, which literally changes how you feel. When the Bible discusses the heart, it is almost never talking about our physical blood-pumping organ. Instead, it refers to the second component of the mind—the deeper level of thinking.

When thoughts leave our head and become convictions of our heart, we often see our attitudes shift. When our prayers and desires begin to impact the emotional part of our being, we may see our lives being conformed to the image of Christ. Heavy, intense laughter is often accompanied by tears, sometimes called tears of joy because the deeper part of your inner man is triggering the emotional response of tears. In the same way that tears accompany joy, they also accompany anger. Sometimes when we are provoked, we respond by getting angry or upset; sometimes to the point where our tears well up, and we release that anger or even rage.

It could easily be said that tears are an indication that one's emotions have reached their peak level. Once you begin to experience these strong emotions, you may begin to see the supernatural move towards you whether positive or negative. If that feeling is intense enough and you hold that emotion long enough (in your heart), you will begin to see the manifestation of that thing quickly come to pass.

> *"So the LORD sent venomous snakes among the people, and many of the Israelites were bitten and died."*
> —**Numbers 21:6,** *Berean*

The account of the venomous snakes shows us that even after God delivered the Israelites and did many amazing things in their lives, they stubbornly continued to complain. They constantly murmured and complained about God and Moses in Numbers chapters 11 and 14. This is illustrative of the disposition of their hearts.

The Israelites had ungrateful hearts towards the Lord, as demonstrated by their chronic complaints. God manifested many judgments because of their illicit behavior. For example, in one case the Israelites were being negative and complaining, and God consumed some of the camp with fire as a result of their negative hearts (Num 11:1). Later, they continued to be negative and the Lord sent a plague to spread and kill some of the Israelites (Num 14:11-12). A third time, they complained and God sent snakes among them, and many died from the venomous bites (Num 21:4-9).

Snakes often represent evil or the devil, so a negative ungrateful heart opens a door for the demonic realm to operate in your life, which God will sometimes use to correct or discipline you. Unfortunately, this was the pattern with Israel many times. The good news is that if that proposition is true, then the opposite is also true. A grateful heart that focuses on righteousness and searches out the blessings and goodness of God in all things will open up the door to angelic realm and for heaven to invade your life!

To reiterate, when speaking of tears, I am by no means claiming that we may manipulate God by producing tears. In other words, because you understand the way that tears play a vital role in heaven moving on your behalf, you may not intentionally force yourself to cry because you believe that God is obligated to respond because you cried. That is not the message that I'm presenting.

Rather, it is when tears are coupled with faith, or belief, or a deep emotion that we begin to see a supernatural response. God cannot be manipulated, and He knows the heart. My endeavor is not to teach you to force out tears because you need a prayer answered; my goal is to get you to embrace the tears that come naturally, and to know that heaven responds favorably to your pain. Tears are not wasted, and they are precious to God. We will see how much He values them throughout the duration of this book.

2.
Is God Moved by Emotion or by Faith?

The title asks a provocative question. But is the answer so obvious that the question is ridiculous? Most people would quickly respond, "God is only moved by faith!" I have heard preachers become so animated on this point that they shout, "GOD IS NOT MOVED BY YOUR TEARS, HE'S MOVED BY YOUR FAITH!!"

I admit, when I used to hear that preached it made sense, based upon Scripture and the mechanics of the Christian life that, *yes*, God is only moved by our faith! But even still, something didn't quite sit right with me. I would consider my relationship with my own parents, and although they were concerned with what I believed, they were also profoundly concerned with my tears and my pain.

Scripture often compares God's relationship with believers like the parental relationship that we have with our own children (Luke 11:13; Matthew 7:11). Now that I am a dad to two healthy, amazing children, my understanding about how God loves us has only deepened. This is quite opposite of the strict religious environment in which I was raised. We were Pentecostal, and our expression of faith was full of rules, legalism, and judgment.

Like many people, our view of God was largely shaped only by law, and how God functioned in the Old Testament. It was as if we didn't get the memo that a New Testament had been established, or that as Christians we lived under a dispensation of grace and truth. Instead, we lived for God based only upon fear. My internal view of salvation was I have to do certain things or else God will judge me and kill me.

When I gave my heart to the Lord, I was 9 years old, and I remember my mom asking me, "Why do you want to be saved?" I literally told her it was because I didn't want to go to hell. Now some would argue that it does not matter *why* you got saved, as long as you got saved. I would say I agree, and although I am thankful that I gave my heart to Jesus, our relationship should never be solely based upon fear. Ultimately, I would have to grow into a love for God, and I would have to be recalibrated in my thinking and learn who He really is, and what His views of me as His child really are.

This understanding came through a relationship with the Holy Spirit, and it truly came from being liberated through the Word. You never want any relationship to be solely fear-based, because that is not a genuine relationship.

I know many believers who have been walking with God now for 20, 30, or even 40 years, and if you were to ask them why they serve God, they will proudly and quickly say, "Because I'm afraid of going to hell." That is a big problem, and it is not the will of God for His children to be terrified of Him, as if He will destroy them if they make Him mad. Don't get me wrong; God is a righteous judge, and God will certainly correct our lives when we're disobeying. Even though God uses things to discipline us, though they might feel like pain or trouble, we need to realize that this is all rooted in love for us. God's chastisement exists so that we can reach our greatest potential.

> *"My dear child, don't shrug off God's discipline, but don't be crushed by it either. It's the child he loves that he disciplines; the child he embraces, he also corrects."*
> **—Hebrews 12:6-9, *The Message***

This verse shows us that we must understand God's heart towards His children. He doesn't take pleasure in punishing us. He doesn't get off on His kids having pain. God is a good God, and He wants us to be whole and happy and to bring glory and honor to Him.

> *"For He does not afflict from His heart or grieve the children of men."*
> **—Lamentations 3:33, ESV**

God doesn't afflict from the heart, meaning it is never His desire or agenda to cause us pain. He takes no pleasure in disciplining His children or judging the wicked. Likewise, I have never seen a good parent take pleasure in chastising or disciplining their children. When we were younger, my sister and I used to get spankings from our parents, and they were pretty intense. We didn't see the benefit of them at the time, but now as adults, we can see why some of that discipline was necessary, and how it had a positive impact on the direction of our lives.

Oftentimes, my mom would remind us, "This is gonna hurt me more than it hurts you." As I child, I had no clue what she was talking about. Now, as a parent myself, I completely understand it. When I have to spank my daughter because of her bad decisions or rebellion, it breaks my heart to carry out the discipline or correction. A spanking is my last resort, and I have absolutely no desire to do it, but I know that it is necessary. But like the verse we discussed above, I would never afflict my children from my heart.

My view of God began to shift based on my experience as a parent, and my understanding of Scripture (such as the parable of the prodigal son). I started to view God as a loving Father, an image to which I could totally relate because I've always had a great relationship with my own dad. I started to call God "Daddy God" because I came to believe that He was even more loving, more caring, and more concerned for my well-being than my earthly father.

Once my perspective of God shifted in this way, my life began to be completely transformed. Fear departed and now it was not at all the motivating factor for my salvation. If you asked me why I gave my heart to Jesus, "being afraid of hell" would not be a part of the equation. Fear is not my motivation—love is. If you cannot say that from the bottom of your heart, it's because you don't know Him.

I know that sounds harsh, and perhaps even judgmental, but allow me to explain. It is not because there was a time when I thought I knew Him, but I really didn't know Him. The word "know" in Scripture implies an intimate relationship. For example, "Adam *knew* Eve and conceived Seth" (Gen 4:1), or "Cain *knew* his wife, and she conceived and bore Enoch" (Gen 4:17). Today I *know* God because I have an intimate loving relationship with Him.

I can honestly say that if hell didn't exist (although I believe it does), I would still be a Christian, and I would still serve God because I love Him. Consider your reaction if your daughter got caught up in a relationship that became abusive. If her husband beat her, blackened her eyes every night, spit on her, and was demeaning towards her, you would be furious if she refused to leave. You might question her sanity for staying. You might make every effort to provide for her escape: route her money, supply a ride, and promise her safe refuge.

It would baffle you if she refused the offer and went back to the abusive husband, because "I'm afraid if I leave him, he'll kill me." Nothing could shatter your heart more as a parent, and you would undeniably say to her, "Baby, that's not real love, and that's not a real relationship. If you're staying with him solely based on fear, then he doesn't love you."

This same principle is true for our relationship with God. I believe that it breaks God's heart that His own children may be terrified of Him, and they think of Him like an abuser who will kill and punish them if they leave. *This is not a real relationship with God.* If hell was not real, I would still be a Christian because I am deeply in love with God.

> *"Love will never invoke fear. Perfect love expels fear, particularly the fear of punishment. The one who fears punishment has not been completed through love."*
> —**1 John 4:18, *The Voice***

Consider the verse above. I think this further establishes how our relationship with our own children parallels our relationship with God. My child's tears impact me in a deep way. Every parent knows their own child's cry. Although some cries are manufactured merely for attention, there is a cry of distress that will immediately move me to swift action.

When my 2-year-old daughter Khloe started to realize that her parents come running whenever she cried, we had to develop some discernment on our part so we were not manipulated by her tears. God is no different. You cannot manipulate God into moving on your behalf by your emotions. But, when you are in distress calling out to the Father with a broken heart, God will move so quick on your behalf, it'll make your head spin!

As a kid, there were times when I would lightly hurt myself—an ordinary bump or scrape—and I would go show it to my parents. If I managed to get their attention, they could discern that I wasn't in major distress and brush it off. They would say, "Go wash it off," or "Put some peroxide on it, and you'll be okay." Sometimes I would actually have a more severe injury, but because my pain tolerance was high, they saw my lack of reaction as an indication that the injury wasn't severe. That is, of course, until I explained what the issue was.

In one memorable incident when I was about 8, I mutilated my fingers. They were repeatedly smashed in an iron door. The flesh was hanging off, my nails were gone—it was a bloody mess. When this happened to me, I was inside and my mom was outside, but I called out to her with that terrifying distress call that every parent knows. This cry was loud, and full of strong tears and weeping. It was as if my mom supernaturally appeared. She came to me quickly, swooped me up, and took me to get my fingers treated. Her response was almost instant because of the level of distress that I was in.

This is *exactly* how God responds to His children! When God knows that His child is in a high level of anguish, He will move quickly and come to your rescue! Most people can relate to being in some sort of distress— let's say a car accident, for example. Many people in that moment of trouble have conjured up their deepest emotional heartfelt cry, "JESUS!" and instantly, the trouble of the situation is abated.

God releases angels so that the car suddenly stops; there is no pileup on the highway while going 80 mph, and they walk away with no scratches, no bruises, and no broken bones. Everyone is astonished and says, "There is no way that you should have walked away from that!" This occurred because in that moment of desperation, God's child prayed just one word with a level of passion and intensity that would not normally be used while praying 10,000 other words.

Effective prayer is not based off a multiplicity of words. One word released in a state of passion, desperation, sincerity, and a deep emotion carries more weight in the spirit than one million empty words. If only we could pray to God daily out of that place of desperation, hunger, certainty, and passion! We literally would live under an open heaven with the weight and government of God on our shoulders!

God is moved by your faith, and God is also moved by your emotions. Emotions and faith are inseparable companions. Our faith triggers our emotions—they are both interconnected. Just like the time when I cried out very emotionally to my mom, I had the faith that she would fix the situation. My emotions were extremely potent because of the level of distress I was in.

It is natural for us to go through events or to have experiences, positive or negative, that affect us emotionally: a loved one passing, a bad report from a doctor, a child not doing well in school, problems with our job, or issues in our marriage. The same is true in a positive way. Once some positive event happens it affects us emotionally: a job promotion, a new house, a new car, or a financial breakthrough!

When those things happen, it ignites an emotional response within us—we laugh, we cry, we get excited. This is because our lives are based on sensory inputs which we can see, touch, taste, feel, and smell. But, as believers, we are called to live supernatural lives, so we should not allow our lives to be governed by the things of physical realm because we understand that the spirit realm is the causal realm.

> *"Faith is the assurance of things you have hoped for, the absolute conviction that there are realities you've never seen."*
> — **Hebrews 11:1, *The Voice***

As believers, if we are going to be whole, healthy, and emotionally stable, we cannot let outside stimuli dictate our emotional well-being. In other words, our joy, our peace, our goodness, and our happiness should not be based upon what is happening around us. Of course, this is the norm for most people, but as Christians we must be different. If we let the things in the physical world affect our internal well-being, we will be on an emotional roller coaster that will attract more of the things we don't desire.

In Romans 1:17 we read that "the just shall live by faith." When you live by something, then it becomes your lifestyle. Therefore, I live a supernatural life and my convictions are not based on anything detectable by my natural senses. My belief system, and what shapes my reality, is based upon the word of God, and my emotions are triggered because I have confidence and assurance in what God says that I can have. So even though things in the natural realm are falling apart, I am not moved by it because I know what God has already promised me. When I remember this, I begin to have an emotional response based upon the blessings that are about to invade my current situation. My faith is about to manifest, and the negative things before me are about to come to an end.

When you really understand this principle, you will begin to capture the feeling of the goodness you're expecting before it actually materializes because you are persuaded that it exists in the unseen world. I love The

Voice's translation of Hebrews 11:1, which describes "the absolute conviction that there are realities you've never seen." You cannot sway me from the goodness of God's promises, so if I get a bad doctor's report and they tell me that I have cancer, I will never react negatively about that. That is because that report is not God's promise for my life; healing and wholeness is my portion. Someone may be saying, "That's easier said than done. He's never had cancer." This is true, but I have had sickness, and I've seen the principles of God's Word work for me and my family countless times.

Most recently in December of 2018, I fell terribly ill as a result of not properly taking care of my body over an extended period of time within my pursuit of the Lord. I was on my way to a church conference in Florida, and before my airplane landed, I felt myself extremely weak and as though I was losing consciousness. The last thing that I remember was my anxiety rising as I began to lose control of my bodily functions. I started to shake my wife to alert her that something was wrong. I regained full consciousness in a hospital bed, only to hear the doctor literally cursing me out about how stupid I was for allowing my body to get in this condition. He began telling me all of the negative things that would/could happen as a result of this incident.

Every time he spoke something negative, I never received it, nor did I let it get into my heart. I didn't believe it because according to Hebrews 11:1, I had an absolute conviction that I was completely healed regardless of the symptoms or the doctor's level of expertise. He that said I could have a heart condition, kidney failure, or respiratory distress. He even told me that I would have to be treated as an inpatient, and that there was no way I was going home that day.

In the midst of all of those word curses, I held fast to my convictions. Yes, I call them "word curses" not to demonize the amazing work of doctors, who are our friends and God uses them, but because the enemy will use those negative words as a weapon against us. The enemy tries to evoke fear, panic, anxiety, and unbelief in order to attack you mentally to open a door for those diseases to come into your body. Taking the doctor's diagnosis to heart is idolatry because you are elevating what they have said over what God has said, and this is sin which opens the door to a spirit of infirmity.

As the doctor began to give me the diagnosis, I told him boldly that I would not have any of those conditions or any negative side effects, and that I was going to walk out of the hospital that day. He laughed, thinking I was delusional, but I said, "No, I'm a Christian." Some people say those things because they know the right things to say, but I was just speaking from my heart.

I honestly never felt worried about my diagnosis. I never felt panicked, and I knew that I would suffer no loss from this event. Within three hours, everything began to supernaturally turn around. My numbers were being regulated at an accelerated rate, I regained physical strength, and within 4 hours I was discharged. I even found the doctor and waved goodbye to him!

The hospital staff told me that my body would not tolerate food for a while, so that I should just eat applesauce, soups, and Gatorade, but after discharge I went straight to Red Lobster and ate a normal meal with no adverse side effects or relapse! God is amazing.

Later that week, I began to experience negative symptoms of what they spoke over me: sharp chest pains, chest tightness, and shortness of breath. I ignored it. I renounced it, and I replaced it with the Word of God. "I AM HEALED, by the stripes of Jesus Christ! I AM WHOLE in JESUS NAME!" As I stated before, the doctors are our friends because they let us know what's going on in our bodies and how to pray. After explaining my symptoms, I underwent several tests, chest X-rays, and an EKG which came back abnormal.

For over 10 months the symptoms persisted, and I was often unable to take a deep, satisfying breath. I never panicked; I never had any fear; I never had a pity party. I continued to do everything as usual, went to the gym and ran 6 miles, continued to preach weekly just as I normally did. And I just kept confessing the Word and thanking God for my healing. I would say, "Devil, you can't stay here. This house is already occupied, and it's filled with the Holy Spirit. Jesus already paid the price for my healing." It seemed like in those moments of confessing and praying, the sickness would manifest greater, but I didn't waiver because I had a conviction about my healing, and I knew it was only a matter of time before my physical body caught up to the reality that I was already healed.

In August of 2019, I was given a clean bill of health. All tests were normal, and all of my symptoms were gone. This happened because I refused to give into the dictates of the enemy. My faith was tested, but I would NOT concede to the negative report. I prayed, I believed, and I rested in God's assurance and in His promises!

> *"Don't be pulled in different directions or worried about a thing. Be saturated in prayer throughout each day, offering your faith-filled requests before God with overflowing gratitude. Tell him every detail of your life, then God's wonderful peace that transcends human understanding, will make the answers known to you through Jesus Christ. So keep your thoughts continually fixed on all that is authentic and real, honorable and admirable, beautiful and respectful, pure and holy, merciful and kind. And fasten your thoughts on every glorious work of God, praising him always."*
> — **Philippians 4:6-8, *The Passion Translation***

This verse provides a good explanation of the power of emotions, and how they play a vital role in answered prayers. This book will dive more into tears as the chapters unfold, but right now our focus will remain on the power of emotions and how God tells us to use them in effective prayer.

Jesus tells us to be in control of our emotions. Do not let adversity or negative circumstances knock you off course. He specifically tells us not to be pulled in various directions, and that in Christ we should have our grounding. Some people might say, "Well, you don't know what's happening with my kids. You don't know my doctor's report. You don't know the condition of my marriage." God says that the circumstance does not matter; there is no reason on earth to be "anxious," or "worried," or pulled in 100 different directions emotionally. He says that instead of letting it get to the point of worry and anxiety, immediately take the issue to God in prayer. Let your life be saturated, soaked, and drenched in prayer.

Now a lot of people's prayers are like pity parties, meaning they speak like a victim and say, "Why me? I don't deserve this." But the Scripture says that we should let our requests, our needs, and our believing be made known unto God, but then He gives us a key principle! *Let your request be coupled with the emotion of appreciation, and thanksgiving, and overflowing gratitude*!

This is amazing! It would be hard to be thankful when the doctor just delivered you a death sentence, right? God says do it—be faithful no matter what! That prayer, combined with your overflowing gratitude, releases God's supernatural power in your life. You cannot afford to get into a low place. You cannot afford to take on a spirit of heaviness (depression). The remedy that God gave us for a spirit of heaviness is praise (Isaiah 61:3).

Someone may say, "Well, I know that God said to be thankful in the midst of adversity, so I'll thank Him." That won't work unless it comes out of the abundance of your heart. This type of emotion must be in your belief system.

As the Scripture stated earlier in Hebrews, this type of faith begins to respond in a highly positive way because the Word of God is more real to you than any negative diagnosis or adversity. You are so persuaded in the Word of God, and in the promises of God, and in the will of God, that nothing can break your flow. (You're about to get your flow back!) You are so fully persuaded in God's truth that it becomes the only thing that is relevant or that matters to you. You only see the world with spiritual eyes now, so natural things will not move you. Watch what continues to unfold after this prayer and thanksgiving—it will be a supernatural peace that is far beyond any human comprehension.

I came face-to-face with this peace one time in my life, when I met Jesus in an out-of-body experience. Before this experience, I thought I had experienced this peace when we lost our first child. God gave me peace when I lost family members and friends to death. God gave me supernatural peace, and maybe I had received touches of that peace, but when I met Jesus it was full blown.

My Encounter With Jesus

I had been in heavy pursuit of the Lord and I just wanted more of God, and I began to listen to some of the great healing evangelists and revivalists who have already passed like Smith Wigglesworth, Kathryn Kuhlman, Maria Woodworth-Etter, A.A. Allen, J. Alexander Dowie, and William Branham. I also started to listen to some of the generals of this generation like Bill Johnson, Heidi Baker, Randy Clark, and so many others.

God led me to a show called *Sid Roth's It's Supernatural* and my faith was ignited in hearing so many testimonies of how God is still moving, and still using so many people to carry the gospel not only in words, but in demonstrations and power.

One thing that I noticed was that many of these people who were very ignited for God had encounters with Jesus either in dreams, or in visions, or through out-of-body experiences. Some even recounted physical experiences. This created a hunger in me, and I said, "God, I love you and I've never met you. If this is true, please visit me."

I began to study the Scriptures, and the revelation of the Word began to unveil to me that it was possible for the Lord to appear to me. I was inspired by reading of how Jesus showed up in the fiery furnace with the 3 Hebrew boys, how King Nebuchadnezzar saw a fourth man that he was able to identify as the Son of God, before His incarnation (Dan. 3:25).

I also read about how Saul encountered Jesus, and the power of God knocked him off his beast (Acts 22:3-16); and how the Lord appeared to Ananias in a vision (Acts 9:10); and how Jesus appeared to over 500 people while in His glorified, post-resurrection body (1 Cor. 15:1-22). I also recalled how God walked and talked with Adam face-to-face in the Garden of Eden (Gen 3:8), and I believe that the blood of Jesus has brought us back to the dominion Adam lost, which includes the level of intimacy that Adam had.

So this revelation ignited a deeper level of hunger within me, and I prayed one of the most sincere prayers I could pray. I said, "God, I really need more of you. Please appear to me like you've done for so many people in the Bible and in this generation. Set my soul on fire for you. Please do it for me, Lord. You are no respecter of persons."

Tears began to stream down my face and I began to worship God. I had such a deep conviction that Jesus was going to appear to me. I didn't know when or where or how, but I believed it would happen! I was looking for Him to show up anytime, and I was excited (and a little scared) so I asked God to prepare my heart, and asked that He come in a way that I could receive.

Within about 3 weeks, I was very tired from working a 12 hour shift, and all I could think about was getting some sleep because I had to be ready to preach in just 4 hours. That particular Sunday, February 11, 2018, I went to bed as normal, and I immediately had several dreams—all spiritual dreams.

I remember having the sensation to go to the bathroom only an hour after I laid down, which was very unusual. However, I got up and thought nothing of it. I remember that I put my feet on the floor of the guest bedroom, where I went to bed after working 3rd shift so I did not disturb my wife's sleep.

I walked to the door and reached for the door knob, but before I could touch it, I flew back like an explosion went off. I literally flew through the air— completely airborne—and when I hit the floor flat on my back, I saw nothing. When I hit the floor, I knew it was the power of God. Somebody asked me if it hurt when I hit the floor, and I said that it felt like I landed on a bed of feathers; it was the sweetest place I'd ever been.

While still lying down, I collected myself and opened my eyes. I remember the first thing that I noticed was that I heard beautiful string instruments and an angelic choir singing the most beautiful praises to God. These were not words, but rather melodies, and they were holding these notes.

At that moment, I remember feeling an indescribable peace. This peace was real and tangible; it was so potent that I felt like it was a literal person that I could reach out and grab. The air molecules were infused with peace.

I felt like I could have experienced everything Job went through in that moment, and it wouldn't have even phased me (literally)! This was something that I never had experienced; it surpassed all human comprehension; it was unfathomable!!

As I was taking it all in, I began to sit up, and as soon as I did, I looked in the direction of the door and immediately saw Jesus! He had His back to me. He was standing around 6 feet tall and He had on a white robe, with long brown wavy hair.

I immediately knew in my spirit that this was Jesus. So I called out, "JESUSSSSSSSSSSSSSSS!!!!"

The first thing that I noticed was that my mouth didn't move. I was telepathic. My voice came out of my spirit and when I called him, He turned around. He reached His hand out to me as I was on the ground, and I grabbed His hand. It felt like warm flesh and bones.

All I could say was, "THANK YOU!" This 'thank you' was from the sentiment of my heart. Then I rephrased it and said, "THANK YOU FOR EVERYTHING!" I thought about my salvation, His sacrifice, my kids, my family, my health, my life, everything! He looked at me and said, "I LOVE YOU!"

This statement penetrated my soul; there are no words to describe His love for us. All I can say is that when He looks at you, you know and understand that He knows everything about you—the good and the bad—but His love is unwavering and it's deep.

Those words shot straight through me, and every part of my body responded to His love and His presence. I had goose bumps. The hairs on my arms were raised. Even my eyelashes and eyebrows were at attention; they knew this was their creator.

Jesus's love is indescribable, and I never had a clearer picture than that moment. The love I have for my children changed my heart, and it's very tough to match, but the love Jesus has for us far exceeds that love. His love for us is so great that it truly makes the love we have for our children look like hate.

Jesus turned around as if He was about to walk through the door. I wasn't ready for the greatest moment of my life to end, so I cried out "Jesus!!!" And I sat up and grabbed His left arm with my left hand—I felt muscle tone. He turned around, full of humility, looked at me and said, "I LOVE YOU."

This time it was much slower, much more assuring, and even more potent than the first time. I released His arm and He proceeded to walk out, but turned around one more time and said, "I'll be back." I was in complete shock as He proceeded to walk through the door.

I literally appeared back in my bed (like Star Trek). I started making phone calls but I couldn't even initially speak. I was overwhelmed and in awe of the encounter that I just had with the Lord Jesus Christ.

Not only did this encounter overwhelm me so much that I literally could not speak words, but also without effort tears began to flow out of my eyes. This was a natural response of just how deeply I was impacted by one of the most amazing experiences of my life.

About a month before this encounter took place, in January of 2018, a "spirit of brokenness" had literally come upon me and rested on me for about a month and a half. It was through brokenness, weeping, contriteness, and faith that I saw the Lord in a way I had never seen him. I touched the Lord and He touched me in a way I'd never been touched before.

Looking back on that experience, I remember that my heart was so filled with anticipation of encountering Jesus that there was not an ounce of doubt. I didn't know when or how, but I knew that I was hungry to know Him in a more intimate way.

I was honestly praying for His visitation and habitation, which will be my prayer until I die. I desire God to visit me and stay with me. I want the tangible, manifested presence of God—the glory of God—to rest on me all the days of my life. I want to behold the beauty of the Lord, and inquire in His temple. I was so persuaded by God's Word that Jesus would visit me, and I was filled with so much faith that I knew it was only a matter of time.

Every day in prayer, I would nearly pray with one eye open, just knowing that Jesus would appear or walk through the wall. I prayed out of my heart and I wasn't sad. Just to think about Jesus and what He has done for me would cause an overwhelming gratitude to well up within me. My heart was so tender towards the love of God that I would just weep.

I would also be so remorseful of my sin and unworthiness, that most of my prayers in that season were prayers of gratitude accompanied by severe weeping (hallelujah). So yes, God is moved by our faith, but God is definitely moved by our emotions! Tears are a byproduct of accessing our deepest level of emotion, and when you tap into that level of emotion, heaven has obligated itself to move rapidly in your direction.

Brokenness is one of the most underrated gifts! People look at it as being sad, and they think, "I don't want to be sad. I don't want my spirits broken. I want to be happy and joyful." People will even attempt to get theological and say that "Jesus came and removed the shame and condemnation, so if you're crying that is not from the Spirit of God. The enemy comes to condemn. Christ liberates us, and sets us free and makes us worthy!"

I can agree that there is truth in that way of thinking, but not entirely. This type of brokenness—this level of weeping is something that happens as a result of encountering God in a way that is so deep, so obvious, and so apparent that you take on His heart. Furthermore, to see God for who He is exposes your own humanity, and it causes you to see yourself as you really are.

When I speak of emotion, I'm literally speaking of capturing the feeling of something that you are experiencing. Most people get "emotional" (good or bad) as a result of some literal event or some physical stimuli that has taken place in their life. Some examples include the death of a loved one, bad news from the doctor, being blessed with a million dollars, a raise on the job, marrying your soul mate, etc. We wait for something to happen, and then our emotions are triggered.

With that being said, most Christians live their lives based upon sensory impulses: what we can see, touch, taste, hear, and smell. This is natural. God made us that way in order to want to relate to things that resonate with our physical being. This is why Israel began to make a golden calf to worship when Moses went up on the mountain to pray. Their leader was gone and they felt the need to relate to something physical and tangible (Exo. 32:1-4).

Although that way of living is *natural,* it should not be *normal* for the believer. This applies in the same way when we get emotional during those good or bad moments in our lives. For the believer, it should not take natural stimuli to trigger an emotional reaction. When you believe God for anything, you should cry in the same manner which you would cry if a doctor said that you are cancer free after battling it for ten years. You should cry just because God said in His Word that you are healed. When you asked for healing and rebuked that cancer, you knew with conviction that it was already done in the spirit realm, and it was only a matter of time before your physical body caught up to the reality of that healing!

What I am saying is that it requires no physical evidence for us to be so persuaded, so sure, so convinced of the Word of God. We innately pray with passion, fervency, and security based upon what we know!

3.
Tears Are a Language That Heaven Understands

"Thus saith the LORD God I have heard thy prayer, I have seen thy tears: behold, I will heal thee."
—2 Kings 20:5, KJV

"I pour out my tears to God."
— Job 16:20, KJV

Tears are clearly discerned and understood by heaven. While in the midst of adversity, calamity, and detriment, Job said not only did he pour out his tears, but he poured out his tears *to* God. By saying this, he meant that he knew and understood that his crying was not in vain, and that heaven interpreted his tears as a language and they would be received favorably.

Many readers have experienced such extensive times of testing that there were seasons where all that you truly could do was cry! You would try and pray, but there were no words that could adequately describe the devastation that you were facing. In those moments of grief and distress, all you could do was release the pain through tears and wailing. In a plea of desperation, you simply cried out, "God, please help me!" Those prayers are seen, heard, and received. Job said those tears are sent directly to God, and heaven will begin to move on your behalf just as it did with Job.

One of the ways that we learn about God is through patterns. If we see something occur in Scripture multiple times, we ought to take special notice of it. If something in the Word is meant to be a standard or belief, then the concept will repeatedly appear in Scripture—at least two or three times. In other words, you cannot just take a single Scripture verse and isolate it make a point. But when you can find two or three verses that bear witness to one another, then you have an established biblical principle (2 Corinthians 13:1). For example, Job said that he cried tears to God, but we desire to validate this point with additional Scripture references.

To illustrate just how much heaven understands the language of tears, I want to expound on three biblical characters whose amazing stories display how quickly heaven moved on their behalf, and how tears were a cooperative component to their deliverance, healing, and supernatural breakthrough!

HANNAH

The first biblical reference is Hannah. Her story is written in 1 Samuel 1:1-20. This story is compelling, and there are so many principles that we might delve into, but let's remain focused on the subject at hand. Hannah was married to a man name Elkanah. She was one of his two wives, and she was barren and unable to have a child. We know that in biblical days a woman who was barren was looked down upon; it was a huge strike against her womanhood. Hannah was the fourth woman in biblical history to suffer through infertility.

Hannah deeply desired to have a child. Her story shows us that God is concerned with our human needs and longings which are brought to Him in a sincere prayer. This story also shows us that God's heart is inclined towards those who are weak and the underdog. Hannah's rival Peninnah had borne children and would taunt Hannah and ridicule her for being barren. Hannah was mocked by Peninnah and rebuked by Eli, but heard by God.

God did not chastise Hannah for being discontent. We know that godly contentment is a quality we all should strive to possess (1 Timothy 6:6). However, that does not mean that our human desires, even those that overwhelm us with sorrow, are sinful in God's eyes. He understands our feelings. He knows that "a hope deferred makes the heart sick" (Proverbs 13:12). He invites us to bring our requests to Him boldly, that we might obtain His grace and help in our time of need. God heard the cry of Hannah's heart, and He blessed her with a son, Samuel, whom she would dedicate to God. Samuel would be a great prophet to the nations.

What I love about this story is that Hannah feared the Lord, and she loved her husband. Hannah had a very good husband that truly supported her. Infertility in biblical days was not a small hiccup—it was monumental. However, through her bareness, Elkanah encouraged her, saying, "Why are you sad? Am I not better than ten sons?" (1 Samuel 1:5, 8).

Hannah cried and battled a lot of anguish and grief, until she finally went to the temple to worship God, and there she poured her heart in prayer. It is clear from the text that she had hit a breaking point—a place of desperation. She poured her heart out to God, and she made a vow to God that if He would bless her with a child, she would give that child back to God to be set apart for His service.

In her prayer to God, she spoke of her weakness, her anguish, and her misery. The Bible says that she "wept bitterly," which literally means "strong tears of anguish," or that she was "crushed in her soul." She cried inconsolably; desperately; resentfully; brokenheartedly! She had come to the end of her rope—a breaking point. She had no more options. She poured her heart out profusely to God. Hannah's wailing prayers were so extreme that the priest Eli, who was watching her, could not discern or comprehend what she said. Eli's untimely and uncouth conclusion was that she was a vile, irreverent woman who went up to the alter drunk. After Hannah and Eli talked, he understood what was going on.

This discourse concluded in verse 18, and within only two verses, God honored her petition and Samuel was conceived. Just *two verses later* her heart's longing was granted. Hannah had been barren a very long time—many years—but when she hit a place of desperation and extreme brokenness, she got heaven's attention and her captivity was instantly turned around.

I think it is important to note that Hannah's faith was not the key ingredient in this divine reversal. She believed in God, and desired a child for many years at this point. Her desperation for a child shows that she had become more weary the longer her desire was delayed (Proverbs 13:12). It was as if she was saying, "God, if I don't get pregnant, I'm not going to be okay." We know that God wants our wholeness to be internal, not external. But after Hannah wept bitterly and inconsolably, the hand of God was deployed in her life, and she suddenly received the longings of her heart!

HEZEKIAH

"And Hezekiah wept bitterly."
—**2 Kings 20:3, ESV**

The second biblical character that I would like to highlight is King Hezekiah. This story is loaded with revelation. Hezekiah became deathly sick from some sort of boil that worsened and potentially caused infection to spread throughout his body. God sends the prophet Isaiah to visit Hezekiah to give him a "sure word." This was not one of those conditional prophecies that we so often observe and receive; this was a sealed, definitive prophetic word from God that had no variables in it.

The prophet Isaiah instructed Hezekiah to set his affairs in order, for you will "surely die"—without question, for certain, absolutely—"and you shall not live" (2 Kings 20:1). Hezekiah listened to the word of the Lord, and he didn't argue with the prophet! He *immediately* turned his face toward the wall in prayer, and began crying out to God from the bottom of his heart, and from the depths of his soul (v. 3)!

Hezekiah wept bitterly, just like Hannah did. It was full of anguish, resentment, fear, despair, hopelessness, and helplessness. Those are not typical not characteristics of faith. Faith produces peace, trust, confidence, assurance, and a deep resolve. However, Hezekiah exhibited none of the qualities of a faith-filled believer, but rather acted like someone who was fearful of death, and who began pleading in desperation full of fear.

He began pleading with God. He might have said, "Please, please don't let death have me! God, please remember all of the good things that I've done! God, please remember how I have walked faithfully before you!" Hezckiah was crying out to God. As the King James Version states it, he *"wept sore"*!

Like our previous example, notice how quickly heaven moved on Hezekiah's behalf—not because he followed all the rules; not because he got everything right; not because he was full of faith; not because he perfectly executed the mechanics of faith. It was because he was brokenhearted, broken in spirit, and crushed in his soul. He was so vexed, so desperate that heaven *instantly* and *supernaturally* reversed the pronouncement over his life.

The next passage tells us that even before Isaiah had departed from the middle court, "...the word of the Lord came to him, saying, Turn again, and tell Hezekiah the captain of my people, Thus saith the LORD, the God of David thy father, I have heard thy prayer, I have seen thy tears: behold, I will heal thee..." (vv. 4-5, KJV).

God literally told Isaiah to turn back around and give Hezekiah another message! WOW! God had given a sure word of impending calamity, and within minutes, He overturned the sentence. God not told Isaiah to go back again and give Hezekiah a new word, but even told him why He decided to do this. God says, in essence, that Hezekiah's prayer along, with his weeping, overturned divine judgment, and caused Him to heal him.

The story of Hezekiah is powerful because that same principle is still true today. There is no problem that exists that prayer won't change. Sometimes, when we are facing calamity—a bad doctor's report, a divorce, trouble in a marriage, trouble on our jobs, a lack of finances, discord in our families, or a broken relationship—we concede and fall into a depression, or else we unload our problems to all the wrong people. We think venting is therapeutic, and to some degree it may be, but none of those people have the power to change anything. If we take the problems to God in prayer, *prayer changes everything*! If we're going to unload on anybody, we need to unload to God! Not only will we get to release all of those toxic emotions, but God will actually move on our behalf.

Prayer can change the mind of God. At the outcry of His babies, His children, He will revoke the pronouncement and grant the request. Some people don't like that type of teaching, but it is true even with my own children. For example, there are times when my three-year-old daughter Khloe will want something to drink before she goes to bed. I'll tell her "NO" without any variables, because she is not allowed to have drinks two hours before bed. But then tears will well up in her eyes, and she'll begin to plead her case in her *babyfied* voice. She'll say that she hasn't had anything to drink in a long time, and that she's thirsty. I'll stick to my "no," because it's too close to bedtime, and I don't want her to have an accident in the bed, and I don't want her to stay awake because of a sugar rush. She'll begin to cry loudly and say, "PLEASE!" At the sound of her cry, my heart just melts, and I reverse my decision quickly. I don't deliberate. I don't ask my wife. I quickly change my mind and my decision because that's my child and I don't want to see her burdened or in despair. God is no different with His own children. He loves us, His heart is soft towards us, and He is deeply concerned with our every tear, every pain, and every emotion.

God told the prophet to go give Hezekiah another word after He just gave Him the Word of the Lord minutes prior. By this we can conclude that heaven was unleashed so quickly that Isaiah hadn't even made it halfway through the palace courts when God said to go tell Hezekiah that he will live an additional fifteen years. This passage is so important in illustrating to us just how much responsibility we have over our own lives, and the importance of pouring out our souls to God in prayer.

I think it is also interesting to note, as a sidebar, that God told the prophet to tell Hezekiah to get natural herbs and plants and to create a mixture from figs, and then rub it on the boil that caused the sickness (1 Kings 20:7). Hezekiah seemed hesitant about the method of healing and asked for a sign to know that this miracle was from God. Ultimately, the prophet prayed and God turned the sundial backwards. It is very important to note that God could have instantly and miraculously healed Hezekiah, but instead He healed him through medicine. Some Christians demonize doctors and medicine, but sometimes God works through these conventional methods to bring healing to His people, and the Bible calls this a miracle.

NEHEMIAH

"And it came to pass, when I heard these words, that I sat down and wept, and mourned certain days, and fasted, and prayed before the God of heaven."
— **Nehemiah 1:4, KJV**

The third biblical example of passionate prayer is that of Nehemiah. He was a great leader whom God used to pull off a phenomenal feat—rebuilding the walls of Israel. After Israel had been freed from captivity, their city walls had been destroyed; the town was raided and burned down with fire.

Nehemiah arrived in Jerusalem in 444 B.C., about 13 years after Ezra had returned there. The Jews had been trying to restore the city and rebuild the walls, but they were always prevented from doing it. Once Nehemiah was appointed to his position, he began to survey and ask all the right questions. He asked, "What is the condition of the city, and the people of God?" They responded, "The remnant there in the province who survived the captivity are in great distress and reproach, and the wall of Jerusalem is broken down and its gates are burned with fire" (1:3).

The Jews had tried for over nine decades to rebuild the Jerusalem wall because the temple and city were unprotected. Nehemiah helped the people accomplish their goal by going to the Lord—literally standing as a proxy for Jerusalem. Nehemiah sought God for four months in prayer, with fasting and weeping! **God will always use someone who has a burden for his people.**

What I love about Nehemiah and this story is that although Nehemiah seems to be a devout and faithful man (we are not told of any corruption or scandals in his life whatsoever), the first thing he does as a leader is—he *takes responsibility*! Many of us are in situations where some of the problems are not our fault (inherited problems, generational curses, and ancestral bloodlines, for example)—but they are our responsibility!

To illustrate, notice that Nehemiah came on the scene and the first thing he did is say "Lord, I beseech thee!" (Neh. 1:11). He has an urgent request! He began to fast, pray, weep, and mourn! The first thing he did was to ask for forgiveness!! Remarkably, he includes himself!

Most of us would have said, "I didn't sin, they did!" Most people would have placed blame on everybody else. But Nehemiah says, in essence, "Oh God of heaven, we repent! We didn't obey your commands. We didn't keep your rules!" This confession covers sins going all the way back to the children of Israel when they disobeyed the 10 commandments in the wilderness!

Nehemiah stated this confession with mourning, lamenting, and beseeching God for four months!! He faced a tremendous construction project, and yet he didn't start working on a strategy; he didn't develop a blueprint; he didn't start gathering a team of architects. Instead, Nehemiah pursued the presence of God through prayer, fasting, and lamenting!

Nothing a person does can be more valuable than fasting, praying, and seeking God with brokenness! *Nothing* can get heaven's attention quicker than pouring your heart out before the Lord in sincerity, desperation, and contrition. *Nothing* can cause angels to be deployed and the government of God to rest on your shoulders like prayer, fasting, and lamenting! In Nehemiah's case, God supernaturally released favor and divine assistance, and what the Jews could not accomplish in over 90 years, they were able to complete in just 52 days.

The Woman with the Alabaster Box

> *"Broken and weeping, she covered his feet with the tears that fell from her face. She kept crying and drying his feet with her long hair. Over and over she kissed Jesus' feet. Then she opened her flask and anointed his feet with her costly perfume as an act of worship."*
> — **Luke 7:38, *The Passion Translation***

The fourth character who demonstrates tearful prayer is the woman with the alabaster box, a very popular biblical character. She was a well-known prostitute who chose to visit Jesus when she heard that He was in a particular house.

When she arrived, she walked up to Jesus and knelt before Him, and began to worship Him. Her tears were so plentiful that they saturated His feet—enough to bathe them! This unnamed woman showered tears on the feet of Jesus, and then she dried them with her hair and kissed them.

There is a lot to be extracted from this story. The vial of oil was worth a year's salary, making it an important gesture of sacrifice. In Matthew 26, the people who looked at this woman thought her behavior was extreme and nonsensical. They believed that the perfume was too valuable to use for such a purpose. Instead, they argued that the perfume could have been sold and the money distributed in a pious act like serving the poor. Jesus rebuked them and said that this act would be immortalized as long as the gospel was preached. Their attitudes were wrong for criticizing the woman's hunger, passion, and pursuit of God.

People will sometimes judge you for your tireless prayers, your brokenness before God, your extended fasting, and passion and pursuit of the Lord. They'll judge it and say it doesn't take all of that effort. They'll say that your time could have been better spent elsewhere. They'll even try and evoke biblical theology to make your passion and pursuit of God look foolish! They'll say, "We're in a grace dispensation. Jesus died and freely gave us all things. You don't have to work for what's freely given."

Listen, when you are in love, these acts don't feel like work. I'm so thankful for God and I'll never lose my hunger and my thirst for His presence! Critics view it as *sacrifice*, but I view it as *sustenance*! This is my nourishment; this is my meat; this is the air I breathe. I live to worship God! Who would believe that church people would get mad because of someone else's worship towards the Lord? You couldn't pay me to believe it!

Jesus gave a parable which justified this woman's worship. He basically said, "She gets it!" She understood the love and mercy of God because she was forgiven of so much. Her heart was overflowing with gratitude and worship back to the Father! Her brokenness wasn't because she was condemned or felt doomed. Rather, she came to Jesus with a broken heart and a contrite spirit, full of repentance, gratitude and thanksgiving.

It was her one act of humble submission and pursuing the presence of Jesus that would be memorialized and ring throughout eternity! It is one thing for God to touch our hearts, but it's an entirely different thing for us to touch the heart of God. This woman did, and when we posture ourselves like this woman, we too will touch the heart of the Father!

4.
How to Make Yourself Irresistible to God

"The fountain of Your pleasure is found in the sacrifice of my shattered heart before you. You will NEVER turn away from my tenderness as I humbly bow down at your feet."
— **Psalm 51:17, *The Passion Translation***

As Christians, we are the bride of Christ, which means Jesus is husband to the Church. One of the things that every husband wants is an attractive wife. Can all the men say amen!? I've been married to my beautiful wife for eight years, and she's very attractive to me. Not only is she physically attractive, but her internal beauty exceeds her physical beauty.

Once my wife and I began dating, she found out my tastes and preferences. She now knows me well enough to know there are certain things I find unattractive, and she steers clear of those looks and behaviors, because they are internal and external! I know many of you reading this want to know what they are, but I'll leave it to your imagination.

She has also shared things that she finds attractive in a man, and I try and meet her desires because I want her to find as much pleasure in this union as I do. She wants to please me, and I, in turn, want to please her. It is not that we become slaves to one another's preferences, but rather it is about making sacrifices to bring closeness and intimacy. It is my pleasure to do what brings her pleasure!

As the bride of Christ, this same principle is true. The Church wants intimacy and closeness with the Lord. He is not concerned with our physical appearance. He's concerned with matters of the heart. If we want Him to find pleasure in us, we need to find what His preferences are and what He finds attractive. Now, here's the secret: brokenness is irresistible to God; brokenness is attractive to heaven! To Jesus, there is beauty in brokenness.

> *"The fountain of your pleasure is found in the sacrifice of my shattered heart before you. You will not despise my tenderness*
> *as I humbly bow down at your feet."*
> **—Psalm 51:17, *The Passion Translation***

This verse tells us that a broken heart and a contrite spirit is a *fountain*—or an unending flow or stream—of pleasure to GOD. In other words, it brings God pleasure to see His children broken in heart, crushed in their spirits before Him.

If you continue to look at this verse, it says that God will never despise or turn away an individual whose heart is postured this way. A shattered heart or an afflicted soul is one of the lowliest positions. It displays extreme humility and meekness. It is a cry for rescue, a willingness to have complete dependency upon God for help.

Sometimes, people may think that this is the position we only take when we are in trouble, or when we have an earnest prayer request because we are desperate. No sir! This is to be the daily positioning of our hearts towards the Lord *at all times*! Every single day there must be a complete reliance on God, desperation for God, and brokenness towards God. Our hearts should be like putty in the presence of God. There should be in our hearts brokenness, tenderness, desperation, a desire for more of God, overwhelming gratitude, repentance, remorse, and thanksgiving. This should be our daily posture in prayer, in worship, and in fasting (yes, a fasted lifestyle). **We must make sure our hearts are always soft towards the Lord!**

There should be such a deep yearning for God, that you will not stop pursuing Him until you are completely satisfied and filled with His presence. Then, once you reach that satisfaction, new hunger arises. You cannot get enough of God! He is your daily bread! This is like an itch that cannot be satisfied with anything else but God. The yearning is so deep that yearning is far too inadequate a word. This deliciousness moves into a deep craving for God. Anytime this craving or yearning is truly this potent for God, it will be accompanied by tears.

Again, tears are expelled once you hit the deepest level of emotion: positive or negative, happy or sad. This is not just having an emotional experience, as many people are just "emotional," but rather this deep encounter with God brings you to an emotional place. I know some of my theologians reading this will say, "I disagree. You don't have to cry." I'm sorry, I believe you do (we can agree to disagree). Once you get so deep into this love relationship with God, no one has to tell you to cry. You can be the most unemotional person on the planet, but when you truly ignite this passion and desperation for God, the tears will accompany it.

I was privileged to be on the road with my mentor, Todd Smith, who has been hosting the presence of God at the North Georgia revival for over two years. The most radical salvations, healings, and miracles are free flowing in Dawson, GA, at Christ Fellowship Church. To know the heart of Pastor Todd and Karen is to know the secret of revival. Pastor Todd always says that it is not about God loving us—we know he loves us—but it's about us "loving him well, and being able to host His presence!"

I remember an instance when we were in Bowling Green, Kentucky, and Pastor Todd preached a convicting message on sin. It was not condemning, but a call to purity and holiness. A guy immediately responded to the alter call, and wanted to give his heart to Jesus! This young man cried out with tears, lamenting, and such brokenness towards the Lord that my eyes began to water, and chills began to cover my body.

This was the first genuine conversion that I've seen in years. You don't see people give their hearts to Jesus like that anymore (similar to the tearful woman with the alabaster box)! At this revival, I saw so many healings take place. I heard the testimonies from the individuals: cancers dried up, tumors died and peeled like an onion, marriages were healed, paralysis was healed, unforgiving hearts were healed, people confined to bed were healed, and deaf ears opened. I can literally name them all. But I promise that nothing was more precious than this man in his 20's soaking his shirt with tears, crying out for forgiveness, saying, "I JUST WANT TO BE SAVED. I WANT JESUS!!!!"

This guy created quite a stir, and had the attention of the audience. As he walked to the altar, Pastor Todd met him, and shockingly didn't embrace him and butter him up. He seemed to be glad this guy seemed so genuine. Pastor Todd asked the man, "Are you sure this is the decision you want to make?"

The young man cried out quickly, "YES I'M SURE!"

"I want you to count up the cost," Pastor Todd advised, "and not make an emotional decision."

The man cried profusely, and his face turned red. "I'm sure I want Jesus more than anything else!" he affirmed.

"It's better to not make a vow, than to make a vow and break it," Todd replied. "I want you to know that this is a life-long commitment, and if you're not ready to forsake all to follow Jesus, then don't do it!"

The man proclaimed, "I'M READY; I'LL GIVE UP ALL!"

"Even if it costs you your very life?" asked the pastor.

"If it costs me my life, I'M READY. JUST GIVE ME JESUS!"

In watching this, I was completely wrecked; I was literally undone. You don't ordinarily see brokenness like that or salvations like that anymore. You definitely do not see preachers seemingly trying to talk people out of following Jesus. But in Scripture, we see Jesus do that all the time. He would challenge his disciples to leave everything and follow Him—you can't even bury your father; you can't say goodbye to your family (Luke 9:59-62).

It isn't that the pastor was trying to talk the young man out of salvation; he was letting him know the level of commitment to which he owed the Lord and warning him not to make an emotional decision. This guy was so passionate and so desperate for God, that he was willing to do whatever it took. Let me tell you: heaven met that young man that night! Consider the devotion of David, the warrior:

> *"I long to drink of you, O God, <u>drinking deeply from the streams of pleasure</u> flowing from your presence. My longings overwhelm me for more of you! My soul thirsts, pants, and longs for the living God. I want to come and see the face of God. Day and night my tears keep falling and my heart keeps crying for you."*
> — **Psalm 42:1-3,** *The Passion Translation*
> (emphasis added)

David's desire for more of God was more than he could seemingly bear. He wanted to drink from fountains of His presence. Brokenness like this literally attracts the presence of God. Brokenness and contriteness are fountains of pleasure to God, but His presence is a fountain of pleasure for us!

Do you see that there is a correspondence between our brokenness and God's pleasure? This is a great exchange! God's appetite is satiated through our brokenness, but our appetites are satiated through His presence! As we are broken before the Lord, He is satisfied and comes near us, causing His presence to flood our souls. As we are filled with more of His presence, we are satisfied and our spirits break even more in the presence of God. It is a revolving door.

David said that he was so broken simply because he wanted more of God's presence; he said that he was overwhelmed. He said that he was wheezing, gasping, and panting like a dehydrated deer in search of water—so was his very soul desperate for the living God! He just wanted to see the face of God, which is an expression that really conveys intimacy and closeness with God. Then David writes that his tears kept falling, day and night. *The Message* translation says he was on a diet of tears—tears for breakfast, tears for supper.

Some people may be saying, "Well, I just don't agree that in Christ we should be walking around condemned and sad all the time. Christ has liberated us; He freed us; He took our penalty and judgment. We should be uplifted and rejoicing." That is all true, but unrelated in this context. I will cover some of the theology of that rebuttal a little later, but for now, this has everything to do with remorse, repentance, and getting back to the heart of God. This is about having a deep remorse and sorrow for our sinful patterns. This is about clinging to God and becoming one with Jesus, even as He and His Father are one.

True repentance is turning from our sinful behaviors, and actually bearing the fruit of holiness. This is a godly sorrow that constrains us in order to get the wrinkles out of our garments, so that we can be a bride with which Christ is satisfied. This is about not being "right with God" through justification by faith, but about truly living a life that reflects the image of God. This is about no longer milking the grace train by merely being *positionally right*, but actually being empowered by grace to be *relationally right* with God. Consider the following text from First John:

> *"But the one who continues sinning hasn't seen him with discernment or known him by intimate experience. Delightfully loved children, don't let anyone divert you from this truth. The person who keeps doing what is right proves that he is righteous before God, even as the Messiah is righteous. But the one who indulges in a sinful life is of the devil, because the devil has been sinning from the beginning. The reason the Son of God was revealed was to undo and destroy the works of the devil. Everyone who is truly God's child will refuse to keep sinning because God's seed remains within him, and he is unable to continue sinning because he has been fathered by God himself. Here is how God's children can be clearly distinguished from the children of the Evil One. Anyone who does not demonstrate*

righteousness and show love to fellow believers is not living with God as his source."
—**1 John 3:6-10, *The Passion Translation***

This passage seems like a hard word, but this is about knowing God intimately, as verse 6 states. The church must wake up out of its coma, and get back to the true heart of Jesus. It is not about eloquence of speech, oratorical finesse, or even about miracles. It's about Jesus. It is about returning to the heart of God!

People who can discern this message have been in prayer. God is preparing the body of Christ globally for a great awakening. We are getting ready for the greatest move of God that the world has ever known. Yes, I know that great darkness and great tribulation are coming, but the darker the world gets the brighter our light will shine. We are about to see entire heathen nations lit up and illuminated with the glory of God, completely saturated with the Holy Ghost and a mighty burning fire! Hallelujah!

God is baptizing us with fire. He's removing the impurities and the imperfections. We are in the refiner's fire. He that has an ear, let him hear what the Spirit of the Lord is saying to the Church! Jesus' mission on earth was that He manifested Himself in a physical body in order to destroy the works of the devil. That literally means that the works of the devil are destroyed—not broken, but destroyed! He didn't break sinful patterns in your life, He destroyed them! He didn't break the addictions, He destroyed them! He didn't break the spirit of lust, He destroyed it!

Anything broken can be put back together, and it may start harassing you again. This is why we see so many believers caught in sinful cycles and enmeshed with so many demonic entanglements. The devil is a liar. His works have been destroyed.

If God saved you, then why should you be bound? Make a decision, and say, "I refuse to live a life that is less than what Jesus Christ died to give me!" From this day forward, I declare freedom over your life. The works of darkness are destroyed! Whether it pertains to your ministry, your family, your relationships, your finances, your business, your mind, your body, or your addiction—the works of the devil are destroyed! You are free in the mighty name of the Lord Jesus Christ! Whom the Son sets free, is free indeed!

Do you see? Being "free indeed" means "to the fullest extent possible or available." To be free means *to no longer be under the restraint or the power of another.* Jesus said that when He set you free, He gave you more than that! He freed you to the fullest extent. You're certainly free. You're undeniably free. You're unquestionably free. You're unequivocally free, with zero restrictions, limitations, or setbacks! He freed you from sin! Wow!

If that is true, then how are so many Christians bound and entangled again with the yoke of bondage? Where is their purity? Where is their holiness? We are seeds of righteousness. We come from the loins of the Father. We were restored back to His original intention for us in the garden with Adam and Eve. Everything that was lost was recovered through the finished works of

CHRIST. We were birthed by the Spirit of God, and Jesus was the first fruit of many brethren.

First John 3:9 says that once the seed is within you—God's Spirit—it is impossible to keep on sinning. We cannot; we have no tolerance for sin. It is detestable. We loathe sin. God took the taste of sin out of our mouths. Sin is now disgusting and no longer appetizing. We cannot be comfortable in a lifestyle of sinful behaviors and patterns!

I hear the people saying, "You are being strict; you are being religious; you are being legalistic." I know you have some behavior that you wrestle with—no one's perfect! Listen, this is not religion at all. I was birthed out of one of the most religious, legalistic denominations in the world—Pentecostalism—and I thank God for my journey and for everything that path taught me, because it brought me to this point. I was raised to "live holy" based upon fear, not relationship with God. We were branded with either *holiness* or *hell*. I never even heard that there was such a thing as grace (at least, not beyond head knowledge) until I left that denomination at 18 years old.

What I am presenting is not a list of rules. This is not *legalism*; this is *relationship*! I'm doing this because I'm deeply in love with Jesus. I want to please God with every fiber of my being. It has nothing to do with fearing hell. Yes, hell is real, with fire and brimstone just as Jesus described, and it is taught many times throughout the entire Bible. However, I am not scared of hell; heaven is my eternal home. I am sealed by the Spirit of promise until the day of redemption (Ephesians 1:13-14; 4:30). My lifestyle—consecrated, holy, striving every day to please God—is rooted in faith, hope, and love. Fear is not of God; it's of the devil.

> *"Love never brings fear, for fear is always related to punishment. But love's perfection drives the fear of punishment far from our hearts. Whoever walks constantly afraid of punishment has not reached love's perfection."*
> **—1 John 4:18, *The Passion Translation***

To reiterate the point: if you live in constant fear of punishment, and that is what is keeping you "living right," then at best you're a very immature believer who does not know God intimately. At worst, you need to be converted.

With every fiber of my being, I say today: if hell was not real—if it did not exist, or was a non-factor—I would without a doubt serve God in the beauty of holiness, and I'd run after Him with my very life! Because I'm *in love*! I am obsessed with Jesus; He's everything to me! Getting to the heart of God brings repentance, holiness, and brokenness. This truly comes through prayer, and by soaking in His presence.

Jesus must become your passion. If you start reading His Word, fasting, and praying for any reason other than being in love, then you will burn out. If you do all the right things because they are *the right things to do*, the plan will never work. You will eventually stop doing it, and you'll grow weary. But when you become passionate about His presence, it shines a light on who you are, and you'll repent without being prompted. You will cry out for mercy and automatically be brought to weeping because His light, His radiance, and His glory expose the gross negligence of who we really are outside of Him.

In Isaiah 6, the prophet Isaiah saw a vision of the Lord seated on His throne, surrounded by angels. He sees God in all of His glory, majesty, righteousness, holiness, beauty, and splendor. When Isaiah sees this sight, God does not condemn him. But being in the presence of an Almighty God, the darkness of Isaiah's heart was exposed in the light. Isaiah truly saw himself—all of his guilt, and all of his sin—and cried out, "Woe is me!" It was an acknowledgement of humility and repentance.

Where did that come from? This should be the greatest moment of Isaiah's life! He actually saw God in a heavenly encounter! However, Isaiah instinctively, without prompting, burst out with shouts of woe. God then sent an angel to cleanse him and make him worthy to stand before Him.

There is more to this story, but I wanted to highlight Isaiah's brokenness, repentance, and sorrow due to being in the presence of God. The experience really changed the way he saw himself. Isaiah was a prophet who had a history with God, but this encounter would change his ministry, his life, and his heart forever. Nobody had to prep him, or coach him. Repentance just came naturally out of his heart. He was so humbled; he felt unworthy in the presence of a majestic, holy God, and he cried out from his soul in repentance.

I know what Isaiah felt. About three years ago, my walk with God had become stale. It was dry, and I was burnt out on ministry. Pastoring was not fulfilling me, and I was tired. My own personal walk with God had dried up. I began trying to find the best twists and turns to produce the most creative and catchy sermons, instead of conveying God's heart.

My ministry truthfully wasn't working, and to be honest, neither was my personal walk with God. I neglected my own personal devotion, and the passion and fire was gone in my relationship with the Lord. I was also fed up because we weren't seeing miracles; we weren't seeing salvations. Christianity was so predictable. I was tired of religion.

I remember thinking, "God, there has to be more to it than this." My daily prayer was, "God, fill me again with your precious Holy Ghost. Lord, I don't know how to get my passion back. I don't know how to get my hunger back. Please, Lord, can you reignite the hunger in my soul? Lord, if David wanted a clean heart and asked you to create it for Him, then I believe that I can ask you for a heart that is hungry for you. I believe that you'll create it for me!"

Seemingly, nothing happened for a few months, until one night at work as I was reading the Word of God. The Holy Spirit began to speak to me through Scriptures, which reignited my appetite for more of God. The Word became alive and real in a fresh new way, which is difficult to explain. I'd read these Scriptures before, but it was like seeing them through a different lens. Then, I began binge-watching the show called *Sid Roth's It's Supernatural* for as many as 6 to 8 hours per day. When I heard the testimonies of spiritual encounters, healings, and God doing impossible things in this generation, a new found hope was ignited in my heart.

The Holy Spirit arrested me one night in a way I'll never forget. I remember that I'd never felt the presence of the Holy Spirit closer to me. I didn't visibly see anything like a vision, but I felt like I was face-to-face with God. I was sitting in my chair with tremors—uncontrollable shaking and jerking. I was so shook up, I remember that I tried to open up my mouth to say, "Thank you, Lord." I just couldn't stop repenting. Without any effort, thinking, or prompting, I said, "Lord, I am so sorry. I repent. God, please forgive me. I'm so sorry, Lord."

I began to cry uncontrollably without even thinking. I felt like Jeremiah when he spoke of his head being a spring of water and his eyes a fountain of tears (Jer. 9:1). I literally "wept sore." My shirt was saturated with tears and snot. I could have filled up a 16-ounce cup. As I continued to shake, cry, and repent, I felt God's presence so close to me; it was incredible.

Someone asked me why was I crying and repenting, and told me that I shouldn't feel condemned. But, like Isaiah, that night I saw God in a way I'd never seen Him before. I felt so close to God, it seemed like I was in heaven before His throne. My desk was gone; the table was gone; the room vanished (in my mind). My eyes were clinched, and it was only me and Jesus. I saw a perfect, holy, radiant, wonderful, worthy, and righteous God. It occurred in a way that was so real, so tangible, and so perceptible that His light exposed my darkness.

God never condemned me, but that night I saw myself as I truly am. Although there was no conscious sin in my life at that time, and I've lived a pretty moral life, I realized at that moment that I'm a sinful man. I was so thankful for His sacrifice offered to save my wretched soul. I saw clearly for the first time my unworthiness in comparison to who He truly is.

That night, the term "justification by faith" became alive and took on a new meaning. All self-righteousness was stripped from my soul. I realized how much I really had taken for granted, and that if I never made a mistake from now until I die—and lived sinless—I would still be a debtor.

I could clearly see that although holiness and sanctification are very important for us to live and walk out, we are not holy based on our good behavior. Rather, we are clothed in robes of righteousness (Isaiah 61:10). I saw clearly that my salvation was too big for me; I could never attain it in my own strength. I truly had an epiphany: as moral as I've tried to live, none of that could ever purchase my salvation, and in my own strength I fall grossly short every time. All I could do without thinking was repent. With a heart full of gratitude, and a fear and reverence from God, I literally cried strong tears and lamented. I was crushed in my soul.

Still trembling and weeping, I had my eyes glued shut, and out of nowhere, in a closed vision, I saw the clearest image of Jesus on a cross with his head bowed to the side, and a crown of thorns on his head. I saw the sacrifice of my savior visibly for the first time in my life, and it was the most beautiful thing I'd ever seen. I was almost startled because it was so real and so prominent. I quickly opened my eyes, but then I wanted to see the vision again, so I closed my eyes, but the image was gone. That encounter will never leave me; even typing it out now I'm getting teary-eyed.

It's also important to note that brokenness and weeping are literally a spirit and a gift. Often, we seek the popular spiritual gifts, but you can ask God to give you a spirit of brokenness. The reason why this is a gift from God—not a listed spiritual gift—is because it recalibrates you back to the heart of the Father. Above anything else, that's what we want. We want to be in His presence. We want to love like He loves, feel what He feels, and minister and tend to His desires.

Anytime there is brokenness, God's presence comes near in a way that we normally would not know. In a moment of true, pure repentance and brokenness, I visibly saw the Lord in a vision. It is not a coincidence that He appeared to me visibly in that moment of my deep anguish and repentance. Had I not seen Him, I knew He was there because of the intensity of His presence. Not only does He not reject a broken heart and contrite spirit, but He is near to the brokenhearted.

> *"The Lord is close to all whose hearts are crushed by pain, and he is always ready to restore the repentant one."*
> — **Psalm 34:18, *The Passion Translation***

I didn't ask for it, nor was I aware of it at the time of the encounter, but that night I received a spirit of brokenness. Literally that spirit of weeping was on me, and it stayed on me for several weeks. I could feel weeping and travail. My heart was so tender toward God that I would just cry in prayer effortlessly. I'd cry in church, in worship, in Bible study, in bed, and even in my car. I couldn't stop crying, and I never felt the presence of God so near to me. I remember that within the next several weeks, my eyes were daily full of tears for no apparent reason. I didn't have a paradigm for it, but the presence of God was so near.

I had another vision three weeks after this encounter with Jesus. I was taking my son to school. I was listening to worship music on the way, and I was holding back tears in front of my son. I was just holding his hand while walking him to his classroom, asking God to cover him and protect him. He hung his backpack up. I hugged him and kissed his head, and I sent him into his classroom.

When I stood up and looked through the glass, I saw the entire classroom covered in a cloud. The kids were literally playing in what look like a thick cumulous cloud that just hung there. I thought that this cloud was so strange, because class had not started, and the kids were just running through this cloud.

The cloud was so thick that I could not see some of the children's faces. I said to myself, "They must be doing some sort of experiment, or a science project with dry ice, or using some sort of smoke machine." I went into the classroom and spoke to Jackson's teacher. "Sorry to bother you, but I'm curious what is making this cloud? Where did all the smoke come from?"

The teacher paused, and with a puzzled look she said, "Mr. Snodgrass, what cloud are you referring to?"

"The cloud that is covering this whole classroom," I responded. It's full of smoke."

She laughed and said, "Mr. Snodgrass, there is no cloud."

I was so confused. "Oh, okay. I need my glasses." I walked away so that I didn't appear any crazier. The Holy Spirit spoke to me and let me know that He was near, and that God's presence was covering my son and his school.

God is near to the brokenhearted. Stay near to God. If you truly want more of God's Spirit, and you truly desire a greater hunger for God, then I want to lead you in an activation that will open the door for God to create that hunger in your heart. Once He creates the desire (Psalm 37:4), He will fill that empty place and satisfy your appetite. Follow these instructions and repeat the prayer in a spirit of brokenness.

ACTIVATION

Put on a worship song of your choice; one that really takes you into the presence of God. This can be any song that ministers to your soul and takes you straight into weeping. If you don't know one, ask the Holy Spirit to lead you. Sing and worship God with this song, and worship out of your spirit.

Once you hit that place of weeping, let the Holy Spirit minister to you. Take as long as you need, but in the midst of your weeping, repeat this prayer. Feel free to add anything you feel from your heart. This is just a guide. However, be sure to include the key points of the prayer.

> *"Most gracious and heavenly Father, I come to you now in the name of Jesus, as a son of God asking you for more. Lord, I acknowledge the reality that I don't know you intimately. I desire to know you more.*
>
> *Lord, I repent of my sins, and I repent of becoming so lax in my walk with you that I have stopped pursing you! I realize, Father, that your name is a strong tower. The righteous don't walk into you passively, but they run into your name and you surround them. Surround me, O God, this very moment. Let me feel your presence in a way that is more intense than I've ever felt or known before!*
>
> *Lord, I need more of you! I don't have enough! I want more. I'm desperate for more of your presence! O God, You are my God. I shall seek You earnestly. My soul thirsts for You. My flesh*

yearns for You in a dry and weary land (Psalm 63:1).

Father, I thank you for loving me. I thank you for your patience. I thank you for your compassion. I thank you for your grace! Every day, I will seek your face, and search out your presence with diligence. I thank you that greater glory is here in me right now, in Jesus's name! Amen.

5.
Is It Right to Be Broken?

"The Holy Spirit has explicitly revealed: At the end of this age, many will depart from the true faith one after another, devoting themselves to spirits of deception and following demon-inspired revelations and theories."
—**1 Timothy 4:1,** ***The Passion Translation***

I would like to address this topic of brokenness from a more theological perspective. I would like to believe that everyone will take this message, embrace it, and apply it, but I know that it won't be that easy.

Some people will try and defame it, debunk it, or misconstrue it. Some may claim that I am preaching a works-based salvation, or a message of condemnation. Some may point out that walking in the finished work of the cross eradicates both the need for self-effort and the need for us to be sin-conscious. They would conclude that this concept of being broken is a false doctrine that breeds condemnation, inspires self-loathing, and destroys confidence. To add insult injury, they might also conclude that this view is heretical on the grounds that nothing can be added to the ultimate price that was paid by Christ Himself.

I am not saying or implying any of the above. I am saying that when we truly become God-conscious, we will lose our sin-consciousness because our thoughts will be fixed on Him and we will put on the mind of Christ! Having put on the mind of Christ, we will think like Him, act like Him, walk like Him, and talk like Him. Holiness will become as effortless was breathing in and out; it is who we are.

I know some very impressive individuals who have more experience, longer ministries, or more education. They say that it seems like the right spirit, but when you get into self-effort or works, you can undo the free unmerited gift of salvation. If you try and obtain salvation through self-effort (works), then you are basically taking an Old Testament (law) mentality, and the law cannot be kept. If you try to live by the law, but offend in one part, then you'll be judged by the law and you'll be guilty of it all (James 2:10).

Listen: we are not working for our salvation; we are not trying to earn anything. Jesus died and gave us everything! We have an eternal blood covenant that is intact and irrevocable with the Father (Hebrews 13:20). We don't *work towards* our salvation; we *work out* our salvation. Compare the following two perspectives: (1) "If I live right and serve Him, then God will love me;" versus (2) "Because God loves me so much I will live right and serve Him!" Do you see the difference?

I heard someone else say that it is like this: (1) "Man, I messed up. I hope my dad doesn't find out;" versus (2) "Man, I messed up. I've gotta call my dad!" This call to holiness is very biblical and it is not oppressive; it is freeing. We were not created to constantly toil in cycles of sin. God sent Jesus to destroy that. We were created to rule, reign, subdue, and have dominion over all the power of the enemy.

> *"Now you understand that I have imparted to you all my authority to trample over his kingdom. You will trample upon every demon before you and overcome every power Satan possesses. Absolutely nothing will be able to harm you as you walk in this authority."*
> — **Luke 10:19, *The Passion Translation***

Jesus told His disciples that they have authority to conquer every sinful habit, every demonic attack, and every dark spirit that would try and harass us. It is under our feet! This is not a cliché; it is the literal truth of the kingdom of light! Holiness comes by being in the presence of God; it comes through intimacy, and it comes by the fear of the Lord.

> *"Therefore, since we have these [great and wonderful] promises, beloved, let us cleanse ourselves from everything that contaminates body and spirit, completing holiness [living a consecrated life—a life set apart for God's purpose] in the fear of God."*
> —**2 Corinthians 7:1, *Amplified Bible***

By the Spirit of God, we are entering into one of the greatest moments in history. The earth is groaning for the manifestation of the sons of God to stand up and walk in power, love, and inheritance. Restoration is coming back to the house of God. Just as in the days of Hezekiah, the temple is being restored; like the days of Nehemiah, the walls are being rebuilt. What the church has lost by way of power and glory is coming back.

God truly has saved the best wine for last. This outpouring will be so much more potent than what we saw in the days of the generals, such as A. A. Allen, Jack Coe, Maria Woodworth-Etter, Aimee Semple McPherson, William Branham, Smith Wigglesworth, William J. Seymour, Charles H. Mason, and Kathryn Kuhlman. We are about to see a culmination of what has preceded us up until this present moment. It will make what the generals walked in look like Sesame Street. It will not be an encore, but a zenith, and so much greater than before. By this, I mean no disrespect to the fathers of the faith.

This next move of God will not just be about signs, miracles, and wonders. This next move will truly embody the heart of the Father. This generation will capture the heart of the king, and when you get the heart of the king, you gain full access to His kingdom, His royalty, His rule, and His realm.

Miracles will not be a rare anomaly in which only a select few experience. We will see the glory of God resting on the body of Christ. This will not be a form of celebrity superstar Christianity. As it has been prophesied by many spiritual leaders and in Scripture (Joel 2:28-32; Acts 2:16-18), people are going to start emerging from all over with the power and presence of God. You will see *fire hubs,* or hot spots where the glory of God is manifested in a tangible way, pop up all around the country.

I have visited a few of the gravesites of some of the generals whom I admire. I do this to pay homage to the God that was within them. We don't idolize them or worship them—or try and soak up their anointing (a silly idea). But their lives so deeply impacted me. It seems closer to me to go pay tribute to someone who licked the earth for God, than reading about Paul or Peter. These were people who died in the last 150 years that walked in the power of God.

I remember laying flowers on William Branham's grave. I prayed with my wife that no matter how his story ended, it is undeniable that God's hand was on his life. We cried out for God to do it again in this generation. "God, we honor your servant, and we know that what we honor, we open ourselves up to receive it."

One day, I went to Maria Etter's gravesite after I dropped my son Jackson off at pre-school. I was going to stop by quickly, because it was only 5 minutes from my house. I had been there before, so I didn't plan on staying long at all. I just felt led to stop by that day. I always hated graveyards until I started visiting the graves of the generals.

On this particular occasion, I felt inspired to worship God while out at the grave of Etter. I literally just began to thank God and praise Him; it was just pure gratitude from my heart. I didn't have any prayer request. This was literally just a prayer of worship.

As I began pouring my heart out to the Lord, I started pacing back and forth, worshiping God in English, and worshipping God in tongues. I put on a 6 hour worship track, and I sat down in front of the gravestone, Indian style. I continued to worship God with my eyes shut, and I completely lost myself in my worship to the Lord.

The next thing I knew, I fell beneath the ground and landed on my feet. I remember seeing her casket underneath the ground. It was spacious like a tomb. I went up to the casket and touched it. The bottom of the casket flung open, and her body fell out of the casket onto the ground!

It was her disintegrated bones and ashes. I felt the power and presence of God as I looked at the bones of this great general, whom I admired so much. Then she began to come alive! I saw life coming back to this body and the bones began to shake, roll, and rattle.

As I continued staring, I noticed the bones started reassembling themselves to form a whole body. However, the assembling of this body started from the feet and began to build upward from there. I saw very tissues, cells, sinew, muscle, and skin—similar to what is described in Ezekiel. This went on until I was looking at a regenerated, rejuvenated, and restored body of Maria Etter!

Completely slack-jawed, I came back above ground into my body. I noticed that there was a black beetle crawling on my leg (I believe it snatched me out of the visitation).

I sat there and asked the Holy Spirit to speak to me and He said that He was getting ready to pour out His spirit on all flesh, and that He was going to restore everything back to the church that had been lost—not only the power and glory that rested on the apostles, the early church, and the generals, but also the glory of God that Adam and Eve lost in the fall.

God is about to reassemble His bride, removing all of the fragmentation, and make us a whole body again. What has been dismembered is about to be *re-membered*!

In First Corinthians 11:30, in a teaching on the principles of communion, Paul says that failure to discern the body would result is horrific consequences; failing to discern His body has made "many… weak and sickly among you, and many sleep." If that is true, then the opposite of that is also true. When we *re-member* the body of Christ—when we come together as one whole unified body—many will be strengthened, healed, and find abundant life!

This was the epitome of my vision of the reassembling of Etter's body. It represented that the power of the generals is coming back, and it will return in a far greater measure. This next move is not coming from superstar Christians. The oil is not flowing from the head down; it is coming from the feet up. It is coming from the laity to the leadership, and from the parishioners to the pastors.

This means that no one is disqualified in this next move. God is no respecter of persons, and He is pouring His Spirit out on all flesh! The only qualification is spiritual hunger! God said that if you're hungry, you can eat!

This message of restoration will not be difficult for those in the flow of God Spirit to grasp. To those who are having a difficult time receiving this Word, I uproot and excavate every demonic seed planted within your heart that keeps you from fulfilling God's calling for your life. Let every veil that is blinding you be removed, in Jesus's name. Lord, give them eyes to truly see, and ears to hear you, in the name of Jesus.

Truly, truly, I tell you that God is about to pour His Spirit out on all flesh (Acts 2:17), and whosoever calls upon the name of the Lord shall be saved (Romans 10:13). We are about to hit a wave of God's glory like we have never known before. Can't you feel it? Can't you see it? Can't you smell it? Can't you taste it? Can't you hear it?!

We are about to globally wake up out of our sleep and we are going to awaken to our identity of true sonship! Many have prophesied it, and we believe that everything has led up to this point, and brought us to this very moment. Examine some of these amazing prophesies (below), and consider where we appear to be on this timeline.

> *"We are not yet up to the fullness of the former rain, and that when the latter rain comes, it will far exceed anything we have seen before."*
> —Maria Woodworth-Etter (1924)[4]

---

[4] Maria Woodworth-Etter, quoted in "Maria Woodworth-Etter: Grandmother of the Pentecostal Movement," *Believers Portal* (blog), last modified February 8, 2019, https://believersportal.com/maria-woodworth-etter-grandmother-of-the-pentecostal-movement/.

"When the Chiefs win the Super Bowl, you will know revival is about to come. God is raising up His apostolic chiefs around the nation."
—Bob Jones[5]

"I see a plague coming on the world, and the bars, churches and government will shut down. The plague will hit New York City and shake it like it has never been shaken. The plague is going to force prayerless believers into radical prayer and into their Bibles, and repentance will be the cry from the man of God in the pulpit. And out of it will come a third Great Awakening that will sweep America and the world."
—David Wilkerson (Times Square Church, 1986)[6]

We saw the moves of the Spirit with the generals. People were healed, plagues were stopped, and the dead were raised. They walked in great power and exploits, and the Word of Faith movement really took over where these amazing faith preachers left off. These were some of the greatest orators.

A person can get so ignited and encouraged in your spirit by listening to these principles and taking heed to the Word. They truly taught sound doctrine and opened up a revelation that had never been taught with clarity.

---

[5] Bob Jones, quoted in a meme by Shawn Bolz, Facebook, January 19, 2020, https://www.facebook.com/ShawnBolz/posts/10163333587500657, as well as in Rhoda Gayle, "Bob Jones' Viral Prophecy Claims The Kansas City Chiefs Win Is A Sign Of Revival Coming," *God TV* (blog), last modified February 3, 2020, https://godtv.com/bob-jones-prophecy-kansas-city-chiefs/.

[6] David Wilkerson, quoted in Tom Campisi, "Did David Wilkerson Give a Prophecy About a Plague in New York City Back in 1986?" *Tri-State Voice* (blog), last modified April 10, 2020, https://tristatevoice.com/2020/04/10/did-david-wilkerson-give-a-prophecy-about-a-plague-in-new-york-city-back-in-1986/.

Since that time, God has shifted the Kingdom into a realm of education and knowledge, and the demonstration of the gospel in power has waned. The generals and fathers of the faith did not have persuasion of speech, the enticing words, or the oratorical finesse that we see in abundance today. They spoke in the power of the Spirit. They demonstrated the gospel with signs and wonders which served to validate the gospel.

As I saw in my vision at the graveyard, we are coming into a season where both Spirit and Word will be married. This is a part of the *re-membering* of the body. I am not knocking education. Going to seminary or getting a master's degree is good and beneficial. God wants us educated and able to comprehend the deeper things of the faith, but we must pray that our minds are not covered with man's wisdom.

In the early church, Apostle Paul was an example of someone who was very well educated. He sat in the school of Gamaliel (located in Jerusalem), one of the most noted rabbis in history. The education he received was strictly in his ancestral law, and he was zealous for God. Paul also had broad exposure to classical literature, philosophy, and ethics, and he even spoke in several languages. I believe this contributed to his success and influence in ministry along with moving in the power of the Holy Spirit. Consider this passage:

> *"And I, brethren, when I came to you, came not with excellency of speech or of wisdom, declaring unto you the testimony of God. For I determined not to know anything among you, save Jesus Christ, and him crucified. And I was with you in*

weakness, and in fear, and in much trembling. And my speech and my preaching was not with enticing words of man's wisdom, but in demonstration of the Spirit and of power: That your faith should not stand in the wisdom of men, but in the power of God."
—1 Corinthians 2:1-5, KJV

Even though Paul could have relied on his own abilities, education, knowledge, or eloquence of speech, he chose not to. Instead, he came in fear and trembling. He came in the power and demonstration of the gospel, and he effectively won souls to the Lord Jesus Christ. I think the church should have never strayed away from this method.

Signs, miracles, and wonders were always supposed to be a byproduct of believing in the Messiah. It is the mark of a Spirit-filled life, not some major accomplishment that one obtains after prayer, training, and 20 years of experience. That is why it is so much easier for an unchurched new convert to walk in the miraculous: they don't know "the rules."

If you give your life to Christ today, and you have not been tainted by religion, just start laying hands on people and prophesying. You don't know anything different than what the bible says. Religion desensitizes us to the miraculous, and talks us out of our covenant rights. Miracles, signs, and wonders for the believer should be as easy as taking your next breath.

Consider this last prophecy by the great general Smith Wigglesworth, a man who was documented as having raised over 25 people from the dead:

> *"I see a healing revival coming right after World War II. It'll be so easy to get people healed. I see it! I see it! I won't be here for it, but you will be... I see another one. I see people of all different denominations being filled with the Holy Ghost... I see another move of God. I see auditoriums full of people, coming with notebooks. There will be a wave of teaching on faith and healing... After that, after the third wave... I see the last day revival that's going to usher in the precious fruit of the earth. It will be the greatest revival this world has ever seen! It's going to be a wave of the gifts of the Spirit. The ministry gifts will be flowing on this planet earth. I see hospitals being emptied out, and they will bring the sick to the churches where they allow the Holy Ghost to move."*
> —Smith Wigglesworth, 1939[7]

This prophecy is a summation of what God is bringing in this next move of the Spirit. It will be a combination of everything we have seen up until this moment. With the recent world events transpiring—from the Chiefs winning the Super Bowl to the COVID-19 pandemic—it seems as if the church is truly about to emerge into a third great awakening!

This move will not just be one of power and spirit; this will be a holiness movement. It will not be a movement merely *branded* as holiness, characterized by legalism, religious spirits, self-righteousness, self-works, and dress codes.

---

[7] Smith Wigglesworth's prophesy to Lester Sumrall, quoted in "Smith Wigglesworth's 1939 Prophesy," *Call The Nation To Prayer* (blog), last modified December 29, 2018, https://ctntp.uk/2018/12/29/smith-wigglesworths-1939-prophecy/.

This one will actually be a *true* holiness movement. It will be a movement of power, love, and fruit of the Spirit. People will have the temperament or the character of God, walking in humility and meekness. They will understand their true identity and that they are holy. They will understand the point of conception in the Spirit through the blood of Jesus and justification by faith (Romans 5:1). They will understand that holiness is a work of Jesus, and that He put holiness on us *positionally* at the cross, but the fruit of holiness is a work of the Holy Spirit and it is being pursued daily with fear and trembling.

The fear of the Lord is being restored back to the church—a deep, awe-inspiring reverence. The fear of the Lord is such a deep level of reverence, awe, and wonder. It is not a fleshy fear, as if we are constantly terrified to go before Him, or that we are literally mortified of God. I personally don't feel like God wants us to be scared of Him with an anxiousness or nervousness. That would seem to cancel the whole of His message, which instructs us to have a sound mind, to walk in peace, and that God is perfect love and "perfect love dispels all fear" (1 John 4:18).

Often, when people have encountered angels, they are literally in fear and are scared. There are times that we encounter the glory of God in such a potent way that our physical bodies are naturally overwhelmed in panic, fear, and anxiety. There is literally no paradigm to measure the amount of power, beauty, majesty, and glory that exists in the presence of an almighty God. It is beyond human comprehension. It is foreign to us, because we have not yet been made perfect in our glorified bodies, and our flesh reacts aversively to that. If you have a genuine encounter with heaven in your physical body, you will be terrified.

Encountering God in the Spirit is different, because you are not in your flesh; it is your spirit that relates to God, having already been made perfect upon becoming born again. So flesh encounters are different than spirit encounters. When you encounter God or angels in the spirit—specifically out-of-body experiences—you won't experience that fear. That is how you know the difference.

When you have an out-of-body experience based upon your conscious awareness, you cannot tell if you are in your body or out of your body; it feels the same (2 Corinthians 12:3). For example, in Matthew 28:3-5, the Bible describes the beauty and glory of angels: their countenance was like lighting; they were majestic, radiant, and beaming with the glorious rays. The guards became fearful and fell to the ground as dead men.

Why would such a beautiful encounter with heaven cause these men to pass out in fear? The angels actually had to tell them "Do not be afraid!" One would think that they would be excited and in awe of the beauty of these angelic beings. However, their flesh could not bear it.

One of the major things that this generation has lost is the fear of the Lord. We have a passive, casual, lackadaisical attitude towards God and His being. This is reflected in our worship, in our prayer life (if we even have one at all), in our devotion, in our lifestyle, and in our conversation.

If we truly had the fear of God within us, we would not do half of the things that we do. Regarding godly fear, GotQuestions.org wrote this:

> What does it mean to work out our salvation with fear and trembling? Paul couldn't be encouraging believers to live in a continuous condition of nervousness and anxiety. That would contradict his many other exhortations to peace of mind, courage, and confidence in the God who authors our salvation. The Greek word translated "fear" (*phobou*) in this context can equally mean "reverence" or "respect." Paul uses the same phrase in (2 Corinthians 7:15) where he refers to Titus as being encouraged by the Corinthians' reception of him "with fear and trembling," that is, with great humility and respect for his position as a minister of the gospel of Jesus Christ. Paul himself came to the Corinthian church in "weakness and fear, and with much trembling" (1 Corinthians 2:3), mindful of the great and awesome nature of the work in which he was engaged.
>
> The sense in which we are to work out our salvation in fear and trembling is twofold. First, the Greek verb rendered "work out" means "to continually work to bring something to completion or fruition." We do this by actively pursuing obedience in the process of sanctification, which Paul explains further in the next chapter of

Philippians. He describes himself as "straining" and "pressing on" toward the goal of Christlikeness (Philippians 3:13-14). The "trembling" he experiences is the attitude Christians are to have in pursuing this goal—a healthy fear of offending God through disobedience and an awe and respect for His majesty and holiness. "Trembling" can also refer to a shaking due to weakness, but this is a weakness of higher purpose, one which brings us to a state of dependency on God. Obedience and submission to the God we revere and respect is our "reasonable service" (Romans 12:1-2) and brings great joy. Psalm 2:11 sums it up perfectly: "Serve the LORD with fear and rejoice with trembling." We work out our salvation by going to the very source of our salvation—the Word of God—wherein we renew our hearts and minds (Romans 12:1-2), coming into His presence with a spirit of reverence and awe.[8]

God is raising up a remnant of believers who walk in true holiness, and understand the grace of God very well. They do not abuse grace as a means to be lazy or as a license to sin. Instead, the grace of God empowers us to live holy.

Some people believe that because Jesus died and purchased our salvation, that we just put all of the responsibility on Him, and wait for holiness to manifest. They cite that our healing "was purchased," and that "by

---

[8] "What does it mean to work out salvation with fear and trembling (Philippians 2:12)?" *Got Questions Ministries*, accessed May 1, 2020, https://www.gotquestions.org/fear-and-trembling.html.

His stripes we *were* healed. They pray as if it is done, leaving the individual to walk away yet sick, saying, "Go in faith, believing God."

That is a powerless gospel. In letter and in doctrine, that is correct, but we never see Jesus do it that way! We never see the apostles do it that way! We never see the prophets of the Old Testament do it that way! When they prayed, they got results. Jesus said we would do greater works.

Jesus died for us to be free from sin, and the moment we accept Him, we get rights to that position solely based upon what Jesus did in accomplishing our redemption. He became sin (taking our sinfulness) that we might become righteous (taking His righteousness). Positionally, believers are in a right relationship with God through the blood of Jesus, but some Christians are not maintaining a practical holiness. They are bound in chains, weighed down by weaknesses, and enmeshed in sin.

Do you think Jesus died to make us *positionally* righteous and not *practically* righteous? Of course not! Whom the Son sets free, is free indeed (John 8:36). He came to destroy the works of darkness; He came to destroy the yokes of bondage over our lives. My point is that even though access to this grace of holiness is available, it seems as though most believers die bound rather than "free indeed." How can we explain this?

The reason is that Christians have to make a practice of exercising discipline, fasting, praying, meditating on the Word, and crucifying the flesh. We are to earnestly contend for the faith that was once for all delivered to the saints (Jude 1:3). We have to fight the good fight of faith (1 Timothy 6:12). These are things that believers should do naturally as a part of the daily Christian lifestyle.

We must seek Him in desperation and with yearning. This is not just a one-time prayer! When people are saved but bound by sin, we must teach them, coach them, encourage them, deliver them, and give them tools to overcome the wiles of Satan! The same principle applies to healing, deliverance, and miracles! Jesus paid too high a price for you not to inherit the promise. Refuse to live a life that is less than what Christ died to give!

To close this chapter, I will provide more scriptural support on how weeping will bring us to this point of revival, reformation, and revolution. Weeping and brokenness will be a forerunner of God's glory returning to the church.

When we repent, put on sackcloth and ashes, and pour our hearts out before God, we will see the aforementioned move of God begin to manifest in the earth. The church must be recalibrate, repent, and return to the place from which we have fallen. We must go back to our first love (Revelation 2:4).

> *"Draw nigh to God, and he will draw nigh to you. Cleanse your hands, ye sinners; and purify your hearts, ye double minded. Be afflicted, and mourn, and weep: let your laughter be turned to mourning, and your joy to heaviness. Humble*

yourselves in the sight of the Lord, and he shall lift you up."
— **James 4:8-10, KJV**

In this passage, James was speaking to the church, not to the world. He was saying that Jesus's bride, the church, has been adulterous. They have tried to walk hand-in-hand with the world. They have become infiltrated by worldly systems. They look like the world and act like the world. The bride of Christ is weak and powerless. James wrote that "friendship with the world is hostility towards God" (James 4:4).

Unfortunately, the church has become so relaxed and so anesthetized that she wouldn't know it if a snake bit her. This is not what it is supposed to look like. So many have bought into an unbalanced grace message. The bride is in a full blown identity crisis! Consider that Jesus warned that people will be apathetic at His return, just as it was in the days of Noah:

"The Arrival of the Son of Man will take place in times like Noah's. Before the great flood everyone was carrying on as usual, having a good time right up to the day Noah boarded the ark. They knew nothing—until the flood hit and swept everything away."
— **Matthew 24:38-39,** *The Message*

The people of Noah's generation were completely oblivious to the fact that they were on the brink of disaster. Their heads were in the clouds. All of the signs were there, and they were still partying, drinking, having sex, and living it up. Then, suddenly, the flood came! This is similar to the parable of the ten virgins. Is the church in the same position? Wake up, Church! Do not wait for disaster to hit before you turn back to God. Do not wait until you to lose something before you give God everything!

James says the remedy for reconciliation is to return to God. He says *lament*, which is strong tears, weeping, and being grievously vexed in your soul. This lamenting is not because of physical pain or heartbreak. Instead, weep because you broke God's heart. Weep because you have gotten away from the things of God. He says let your laughter be turned into mourning. *The Message* says "cry your eyes out before God." Lie at Jesus's feet and pour your heart out. Humble yourselves under the mighty hand of God!

Lord, let a spirit of brokenness and contriteness fall on your people right now, even as they read these words! Let a spirit of conviction and deep repentance fall on the body of Christ in real time!

Lord, we repent of our sins. Forgive us of all unrighteousness. We repent as a nation for breaking your commandments. We repent for calling right *wrong*, and wrong *right*! We repent for telling people they have a right to kill their unborn children. We repent for redefining marriage as being anything other than a holy union between a man and a woman. We repent for all our sexual perversions, including adultery and fornication! We repent for not covering Israel as we should! Forgive us, Lord!

James said that the church should be in deep sorrow and repentance. This is not an Old Testament command; this was written to Christians. This is not because they are under condemnation, or that the enemy is working as the accuser. Rather, James is providing the recipe for true repentance. This is a formula that the church needs to invoke! This is a clarion call. Church, arise! Wake up! Repent!

6.
If It Ain't Broke, Don't Fix It!

> *"Put on sackcloth and lament, O priests; wail, O ministers of the altar. Come, spend the night in sackcloth, O ministers of my God, because the grain and drink offerings are withheld from the house of your God. Consecrate a fast; proclaim a solemn assembly! Gather the elders and all the residents of the land to the house of the LORD your God, and cry out to the LORD."*
> **—Joel 1:13-14, KJV**

The expression, "If it ain't broke, don't fix it," is said to date back to pre-historic times, when hand axes were made by chipping stone or flint against a hard object until sharpened. After hours of laborious refining, the axman would have a sharp blade, adequate for cutting. However, in his zeal to obtain the perfect point, he would strike it one more time, thus chipping away too much material and ruining the ax and the hard work he invested. The proverbial phrase is interpreted to be a warning against attempting to add or improve something that is already getting the job done.

Looking at this same concept spiritually, brokenness is a cry for help from one who is humble before the Lord. The word *brokenness* is defined as to be "weakened, fragmented, or disconnected." It means what once was functional is no longer working.

When we are going through our various struggles or having problems in our personal lives, many times we try and fix our own problems ourselves. We try and use every tool and resource available in order to rectify whatever has gone wrong. Some of that may be our independence, but a good portion of that is pride.

Many times, we believers do not trust the Lord to fix our problems, and we find ourselves trying to solve spiritual problems by using natural means. That will never work!

That error is not limited to our spiritual growth or awakening, but may also include our response to financial burdens, spiritual drought, addictions, and even health challenges. Believers often treat God as our *last* resort, when in fact He is our *first* and *only* resort!

Before you grab the Tylenol, pray first! You did not even try to ask God. You are so conditioned to put your sticky fingers in everything—apart from God—until you have made a complete shipwreck that only the Lord can rectify! Recall that this was the error of Sarah and Abraham as they grew impatient waiting for a child (Genesis 16). Do not let your situation turn disastrous; turn to God as the first option!

The woman who had the perennial issue of blood took things into her own hands when she "suffered at the hands of many physicians" (Mark 5:26). Finally, after twelve long years of suffering, she reached her breaking point and became desperate to the extent that she was willing to break the law and risk her very life to get to Jesus. Once she reached her breaking point, her miracle was not far off!

You have heard it said, "You'll get out of that dysfunction. You'll break that habit. You'll end that toxic relationship when you get sick and tired of being sick and tired!" Anyone can reach a breaking point, but you do not have to wait until a life-shattering event occurs before you get hungry enough to see heaven move on your behalf!

Your walk with God is no different. Until you reach that place of desperation, you will never reach the experience of overflowing with the presence of God. You will never get to that place where you are a *glory carrier*, meaning that you carry the tangible presence of God with you everywhere you go!

Reaching these places will come through a relationship with God and is birthed through prayer. You have access to this—just like the apostles and the early church—but you have to be willing to pay the price! Yes, Jesus paid the ultimate price, but you too must be crucified with Him and die to your flesh daily.

Ultimately, the price is your own time spent in prayer, consecration, and worship. The enemy has blinded the minds of believers to think that we simply do not have time to pray for hours and hours, but really we do. One only needs to tally up the time we routinely waste on social media, television, entertainment, sports, shopping, and other unfruitful works. We make time for what is valuable to us. Time spent in prayer is never a loss, but it is an investment.

When you are unwilling to allow your spirit to be broken before the Lord, you are sending a message to heaven, whether you know it or not. This message is that you have your own life under control, and that you are capable of handling it. However, when you pour out your heart to God and lament, you are humbling yourself under the mighty hand of God. You are making yourself abased.

Jesus taught a principle in Luke 14:11 that posturing oneself in humility will trigger God to honor and promote you. Heaven will intervene on your behalf. In the kingdom, the way down is *up*, and the way up is *down*.

Having a shattered heart before the Lord literally signals to heaven, "I need you God. I don't have enough. My life is not working. Please come and invade my life. Please repair the broken places!"

This attitude is the spirit you take on until you reach Jesus. This is raw desperation. Desperate people do desperate things. If you are too short, like Zacchaeus, you'll climb up into a sycamore tree in order to get to Jesus (Luke 19:1-10). You will press through a crowd that could cause you a death sentence. You will crawl on your knees to have your daughter delivered from demons. Even if Jesus tells you "no" and calls you a dog, you will still refuse to be denied and will say, "but even the dogs get the crumbs that fall from the master's table!" (Matthew 15:27). When you get desperate enough, you will obtain your breakthrough, and heaven knows when you hit that place.

Once you are truly born again, you are sealed by the Holy Spirit until the day of redemption (Eph 4:30). You take on the DNA of God. To sin by falling short of the character of Christ does not break your sonship: it breaks your fellowship with God. Sin will cause you to remain in an outer court. Disobedience breaks the closeness and fellowship and intimacy with the Father.

No matter what my son Jackson does, he will always bear my name. He will always be a Snodgrass. However, there are things that he can do to get out of my good graces. If—may God forbid—he grew up and decided to fight me, steal from our house, and get strung out on drugs, then he would no longer be welcomed in my house. I would have to see some serious repentance and deep regret. There must be sincerity to indicate changed behavior before I could let him have access into our home, simply because the fellowship was broken through sin.

This is similar to our own walks with God. We have to stop being so casual, irreverent, and flippant about how we entreat God's presence. When we seek the Lord, we must give Him all that we have. He wants all of our heart, all of our energy, all of our passion, and all of our sincerity.

We pray to God like we are doing Him a favor; like we are blessing Him just because we showed up. We are content to shoot Him a quick 15 minute parking lot prayer on the way to work. Friends, that approach will never cause you to walk in intimacy and close fellowship with the tangible presence of God. Instead, it is possible to get to a point where we carry God's glory with us every single place that we go! This includes in our churches, our schools, our jobs, and even at the grocery stores.

How would you like to experience 1,000 watts of God's glory radiating from your body at all times? That is what the apostles had. It was so powerful that people knew their schedule and routine of when they walked down the streets. People sought the opportunity to get close to them to be healed of sickness by the power of God. That was the reputation of Jesus and His apostles, and it can be your reputation—and the reputation of the bride!

There is a story that Kathryn Kuhlman was hosting a meeting in a hotel, and she had to go through the kitchen basement to exit the building following her conference. This kitchen was full of chefs and cooks, and no one knew this older woman or her reputation. As she walked through the kitchen, she greeted everyone. Then she turned as she was about to walk out the door. Everyone in the kitchen had literally fallen to the ground under the power of the Holy Spirit.

We are too lazy as believers. We are not fervent in our prayer. We are not passionate. We are not expressive to God in action or in our hearts. We want to pray just a few quick words, even while distracted. We pray with our legs casually crossed and eyes open, and then we are confused when there is no move of God. We are confused when there is no glory. Do what works for you in prayer, but it is obvious that what we've been doing collectively as a church is not working.

We were shaken as a nation when the coronavirus hit. This virus shut down most of the world, including most of our churches. Believers were left to shelter-in-place until the virus subsided. We had to make due with virtual church. I loved the shift that took place in the church when this occurred. I know that the church isn't a building, but rather is a company of believers. But we collectively must wake up and understand that Christ died and gave us power over the enemy!

Jesus said that nothing by any means will be able to hurt or harm us (Luke 10:19). When did COVID-19 become the exception to that Scripture (and hundreds of others like it)? We shout on Resurrection Sunday that "the blood is superior!" We say that the church is a hospital, and Jesus is the Great Physician. He heals all manner of diseases, and has never lost a patient. But we were hiding.

We must be willing to challenge ourselves on this point. If we are not walking in that level of power and glory, we need to be in the house. But there is the disconnect. Jesus didn't heal and work miracles "as God." He worked them as a man in right relationship with the Father, completely reliant on the Holy Spirit.

> *"And you know that God anointed Jesus of Nazareth with the Holy Spirit and with power. Then Jesus went around doing good and healing all who were oppressed by the devil, for God was with him."*
> **—Acts 10:38, NLT**

Although Jesus is 100 percent God and 100 percent man, to complete His destiny He willingly laid aside His divinity and picked up His humanity and completed His course. If He did everything on earth as God, then we would have an excuse. Our lives could never live up to His, let alone surpass the works that He did. However, Jesus taught His followers, "You are my disciples and I want you to go further on your journey than I ever did. Everything I do, you do it as well, and will do even greater works" (John 14:12).

When you talk about passionately pursuing the presence of God—giving God everything in prayer, everything in consecration—we just don't. If we are authentically honest, we each would say that we do not pursue the presence of God. We make every possible excuse: "Oh, I'm not emotional. I don't get all excited." But you get emotional at the football game?! You change your attire, paint your face, jump up and down, and yell and scream when your team gets a touchdown. How? Why? I thought that you weren't emotional?

Since you are in love with that sport, something in you craves more of it. It triggers you. But when you go into prayer or worship, we cannot find you. You are lethargic. You won't open your mouth. You will not shed a tear.

Consider this example. Imagine that you were in a group of five people, and someone announced to the group, "God told me to give 50 million dollars to whoever in the group needs it the most. Show me your heart and your need by expressing your passion about receiving this 50 million."

Game on! You would not have to coach or prep any of them. You wouldn't have to coax them to cry, jump up and down, or fall to their knees. You would see a variety of endless passion and expression. Instantly that quiet room would respond in an outburst of passion because they place such a high value on that 50 million dollars, and they know that if they receive it, everything about their life will forever change!

How much more valuable is the manifested glory of God resting on us and in us—the way that it did with Jesus and the apostles? God said He is seeking for worshippers like that. He said that He pours out His Spirit without measure to anyone who postures themselves to receive (Luke 11:13; John 3:34). If we know that God's Word is true, and the presence of God is more valuable to us than anything else, then where is the passion we described earlier?

There seems to be a disconnect. It is not on God's part. He already said the same Spirit that raised Christ from the dead now lives in us. Maybe the disconnect is where we have placed our value. Anything to which we yield our time, attention, and affection more than God is an idol. There is no way on earth that sports, shopping sprees, or even 50 million dollars should provoke a more passionate, expressive, fanatical response from us than the presence of God.

Our nation has drifted so far away from God. We need God. People's hearts have waxed cold. People are turning away from the gospel of Jesus Christ and have opened themselves up to doctrines of devils. The world's philosophy seems to emphasize self-empowerment—that each person is his own God, which is Satanism.

Our nation has opened itself up to many false gods and false practices. In many ways it has drifted from the presence of God reflected in our morals and ethics. We have to repent and turn our hearts back to Him! The list below, formed by Pastor Steven Andrew, identifies twelve sins for which America needs repentance:

1. False gods [Idolatry].
Matthew 4:10, Exodus 20:3

2. Not obeying Jesus Christ.
"It is the duty of nations... to obey his will," said George Washington. Like our founders we have "no king but King Jesus." Philippians 2:11; Isaiah 33:22 & 9:6-7.

3. Not insisting on Christian religious liberty.
We advance the Kingdom of our Lord Jesus Christ, not false religions. Mark 12:30, Galatians 5:1.

4. Apathy of our God-given rights.
"We are created with dignity. You give us life, liberty, the pursuit of happiness, property, and conscience. Genesis 1:27, Galatians 5:1, Acts 5:29, Declaration of Independence"

5. Taking Christianity out of schools.
Help us have the Bible read daily and Christian prayer back in schools. Isaiah 59:21

6. Unholy laws.
You, the LORD, are our Lawgiver. You only bless Christian laws based on the Bible. Luke 6:47-49; Is. 33:22

7. Ungodly government.
We vote for Christian leaders from president to school boards who fear You, protect Christians and our God-given rights, hate covetousness and are truthful. Exodus 18:21; 2 Corinthians 6:14-18; Genesis 1:27; Mark 12:30; Galatians 5:1; 2 Chronicles 19:2.

8. Helping the ungodly in business.
We help those who follow You. 2 Chronicles 19:2.

9. Killing our children by the sin of abortion.
The USA is pro-life. Matthew 5:17.

10. Serving money instead of God.
Our nation serves You, not mammon (money). Matthew 6:24.

11. Homosexual sin [same sex marriage], adultery, and fornication.
The USA is a traditional marriage only nation (marriage is one man and one woman); we believe in sexual purity with no adultery or fornication. Jude 7; 1 Corinthians 6:9-11.

12. All other sin, including ____.
We want to be holy. 1 John 1:9.[9]

Once we have identified that there is an issue, we need to turn our hearts towards the Lord and cry out in repentance for the mercy of God! We all need His mercy!

> *"Put on sackcloth and lament, O priests; wail, O ministers of the altar. Come, spend the night in sackcloth, O ministers of my God, because the grain and drink offerings are withheld from the house of your God. Consecrate a fast; proclaim a solemn assembly! Gather the elders and all the residents of the land to the house of the LORD your God, and cry out to the LORD."*
> **—Joel 1:13-14, KJV**

Israel had a back-and-forth relationship with God. The Lord would bless them, they would be good for a season, and then disobey God. Seemingly they forgot what God had done for them. They would get taken into captivity, and God would deliver them. This cycle repeated several times.

Many times God would call for a solemn assembly, and Israel would gather for a period of prayer and fasting. These assemblies were a time of serious seeking not the arm of the Lord, but the face of the Lord. Biblical fasts originated from being broken in spirit because of a literal tragedy that was so severe people could not eat due to lack of appetite.

During these periods they would lament and pray fervently with heavy weeping until they heard from God.

---

[9] Steven Andrew, "Heal Our Land and Lives by One Year of National Repentance," *USA Christian Church* (blog), last modified 2017, https://www.usa.church/two-months-national-repentance-2/.

From those experiences, they understood that God desired intensity in the pursuit of God on a daily basis. Lamenting and fasting became inseparable companions.

When a devastating plague of locusts brought drought and famine to Israel, the prophet Joel called the people to a solemn assembly: "Declare a holy fast; call a sacred assembly. Summon the elders and all who live in the land to the house of the LORD your God, and cry out to the LORD" (Joel 1:14; cf. 2:15).

It was not uncommon for Israel to come together in a corporate fast. They identified as one people. They understood that if they are going to see the hand of God move once again, it would take an intense level of pursuing His face. Their trials—plagues, droughts, and devastation—caused them to lament, weep, and cry out to God in repentance.

To see national healing, we must turn our hearts to God as a nation. We need a solemn assembly. But don't wait for a national call to repentance before you call a solemn assembly in your heart. Repent; break your heart before God. Pour out your heart to Him, and ask Him to fill the empty places.

Make up in your mind that if it takes forty days of consecration, it would be worth it to see God's glory in your life. Position yourself in such a way that says, "God, I need you, and I'm so desperate for more of you. My heart is shattered, and I am broken!" The moment that you have that level of conviction and determination, your breakthrough is much nearer than you think. God is saying, "If you are broken, I'll fix you!"

Prayer of Repentance for Our Nation

Lord, we come before you corporately and we sincerely ask that you would forgive our sins. Father, you are a holy God that desires a holy people. Lord, your desire was never to be hidden from man, but from the time of creation you have always wanted to dwell with humanity.

Father, we ask for restoration of our nation and this entire world. Forgive us of our sins and the sins of our forefathers. We ask that you would purge us with hyssop and make us white as snow.

Lord, forgive us for every form of idolatry. Forgive us for disobeying your laws and commands. Forgive us for lawlessness. Forgive us for prayerlessness. Forgive us for the murdering of innocent unborn children. Forgive us for sexual perversions and pornography. Lord, forgive us for our weaknesses and our maladies. Forgive us for our shortcomings and addictions. But most of all, God, we ask that you forgive us for losing our passion and our hunger for you!

Lord, one of the most heartbreaking verses is Judges 2:10, which says, "After that whole generation had also been gathered to their fathers, another generation rose up, who did not know the LORD or the works He had done for Israel." Lord, we fear that we once again have become a generation that does not know you intimately! Bring us back to that place of union and communion. Revive our hearts again! Fix our hearts; fix our nation! We are broken! In Jesus name! Amen!

7.
From Brokenness to Fruitfulness

> *"When your lives bear abundant fruit, you demonstrate that you are my mature disciples who glorify my Father!"*
>
> **—John 15:8, *The Passion Translation***

Every single believer should be on a progressive course toward spiritual maturity. Just as there is a maturation process in physiology, there is also a maturation process in spirituality. In the natural context, my kids learned how to crawl before they walked. They drank milk before they ate meat. They cooed before they spoke fluent sentences. It is no different in the realm of the Spirit.

Apostle Paul literally gave a whole lesson on this subject. As Paul wrote *First Corinthians*, he rebuked them repeatedly, but validated their church as legitimate. He called them believers but "carnal"—interpreted to mean worldly, immature, fleshly, unable to digest the 'meat' of the Word. As a result, Paul could only feed them a version of the gospel that they could handle (1 Cor. 3:2).In essence, he said, "I can only give you the milk of the gospel, because if I give you a steak at this point, you'll choke and die." Jesus taught this same principle in John 16:12. He also taught us not to cast our pearls among pigs (Matt 7:6), meaning not to release revelation or spiritual truth to people who are not willing to handle it or receive it. It is of no value to them.

The point is that immaturity and weakness is natural and is a part of our growth process. It is nothing of which to be ashamed, because you are born a baby by God's design. God intended for everyone to start weak but finish *strong*.

The Bible says that Jesus was no stranger to this process. There is not much written about His early life, before 30 years old, but one thing we do know is that he had to grow into His spiritual maturity. I know that bothers some of you. You are saying, "Jesus is God. You are taking away His divinity and teaching Kenosis." I answer: Jesus was human and divine; 100% God and 100% man. He willingly laid His divinity down to redeem humanity. He was wrapped in flesh and tempted in every way possible without falling prey to any of them!

Therefore, when we go through our temptations, we may know that we do not have a high priest who lacks empathy toward our feelings or our infirmities. Every temptation that we could ever endure, He endured first. That is enough to let you know that Jesus didn't accomplish His destiny "as" God, even though He was. He was so much man it was as though He were not God.

"Let no man say when he is tempted that he is tempted by God, for God cannot be tempted, neither does He tempt any man" (James 1:13-15). God cannot be tempted in any way, but Jesus was tempted in every way.

To further expound on spiritual maturity, the Bible says that Jesus "waxed strong" spiritually (Luke 2:40). It also says that He grew in wisdom, in stature, and in favor with both God and men. As Jesus matured physically, He also matured spiritually. He grew in His relationship with God the Father, and the favor of God continued to increase on His life.

This is the same pattern which we are to follow as we grow in the Lord. Spiritual growth and maturity should be displayed in every area of our lives: the power of God, the presence of God, our prayer lives, our benevolence, our character, and most of all, our love! The problem with Christianity in the 21st century is that most finish the way they started: *weak* and *immature*!

Conversion is important, but discipleship is also very important. Spiritual growth toward maturity is the process that God expects of His children the longer we walk with Him. When my daughter Khloe first started walking, she would fall down all the time, but she kept getting back up! She was getting stronger every day. As a Father, I never once got frustrated with her repeatedly falling—I expected her to! Every day she strengthened her legs until she started walking and soon running. Just because you fall, doesn't mean you fail. You only fail if you stay down!

I believe that our heavenly Father has so much more wisdom and discernment than I exhibited with Khloe, and He fully understands our growth process. As she started off, she would fall every 3 or 4 steps and everyone cheered her on (and our hearts melted). However, if Khloe was 10 years old and still falling every three or four steps, we would have to run MRI and CAT scans to monitor her brain activity to see if there was some form of neuromuscular impairment or intellectual hindrance.

The church is the only place where it is accepted as normal for people to stay babies well into adulthood. In the natural realm, everyone would call an issue to a teenager's repetitive falling. But spiritually speaking, we often see people who are 40 years old in the Lord with the maturity of a 2 month old. And they say we're "judging."

A measuring rod is needed to gauge spiritual maturity. It is very simple—maturity is seen by fruitfulness. Not just fruitfulness, but extreme fruitfulness. When there is extreme fruit in a person's life, it is a strong indication that they are mature disciples in the Lord.

Fruitfulness is not one dimensional. Jesus died to completely save us—mind, body, and soul. Therefore, this fruitfulness affects every area of our life. To say that "I'm a Christian with a lot of money because I steward my finances well, therefore I'm a mature disciple" isn't necessarily true. Many people who are not Christians also have a lot of money and manage their finances well.

The same thing applies to health, or relationships, or even character. You can flow in good character, strong relationships, and physical health without being a Christian. Although each of those areas is good and necessary, they do not have a true correspondence to one's spiritual maturity.

Jesus said, "When your lives bear abundant fruit, you demonstrate that you are my mature disciples who glorify my Father!" (John 15:8, *Passion Translation*). Jesus said that God is glorified, meaning honored, when mature disciples bear much fruit. Jesus instructed us to let our lights shine so that men may see our good *works* and glorify the Father.

The supernatural realm—healings, miracles, deliverance, spiritual gifts, salvations—are absolutely key to that spiritual maturity. Some people get nervous or start to backpedal when you speak of these things. "Love is most important," they say. "Love is the principle thing."

Love is essential. You can speak with the tongues of men and angels, sell all of your possessions, and become a martyr for the gospel's sake, but if you don't have love then it profits nothing (1 Cor. 13:3). Jesus also emphasized that love is essential by highlighting the lack of love among those who didn't feed, visit, and clothe others (Matthew 23:35). Many would say, "God, did we not cast out devils and perform many miracles in your name?" Jesus will say, "Depart from me, you workers of iniquity. I never knew you" (Matthew 7:23). The Scriptures make it clear that one's works do not save a person, and yet the most important thing that will last is love.

We as believers have gotten comfortable with the mundane Christianity. We have gotten so complacent, and have become comfortable with a mediocre Christianity devoid of miracles, healings, deliverance and the supernatural wonder-working power of God. Our lives are supposed to reflect the image of Christ. Jesus was the perfect expression of God's love through benevolent acts, but that never overshadowed Him walking in power as well. Jesus walked in power and love, and so should we! You never see Jesus just show love to anyone without supernaturally fixing the situation—never not one time!

Jesus was loving enough to be concerned about Peter's back taxes getting paid, but He was powerful enough to manifest money in the mouth of a fish (Matthew 17:27). Jesus was loving enough to break His sleep to check on the well-being of His disciples who thought they would die, but He was powerful enough to stop the storm. Jesus was loving enough to visit Peter's feverishly ill mother-in-law, but He was powerful enough to heal her disease. Jesus was loving enough to cry with the bereaved family at the tomb of Lazarus, but He was powerful enough to resurrect him from the dead, even after his body was decaying and stinky.

Jesus never let the precedence of love become an excuse for Him not to walk in the power of the Spirit, and neither should we. Jesus had so much love, that when a man was in sin, He pardoned him and said, "Your sins are forgiven." The religious people did not like that and said, "He's a blasphemer," and "He has a demon, thinking that He's God."

Jesus said anyone could *say* "your sins are forgiven," since that takes no more than uttering a few words, but it is more difficult to heal paralysis than to say your sins are forgiven (Matthew 9:5). Jesus commanded a paralyzed man to get up and start walking, and the man started walking. The people were shocked, amazed, and angry. You see? Jesus demonstrated the gospel through the power of the Spirit!

Paul taught the same message. He did not come to entice people with eloquence of speech or amazing sermons with insightful truths. It is not that there is anything wrong with those things, but he came in the demonstration of the gospel and in the power of the Spirit (1 Cor. 2:4).

In this same vein, churches all across the country boast, "We've seen hundreds of people give their lives to the Lord!" Many are measuring those numbers based upon people who uttered a few words called the *Sinner's Prayer* and filled out some paperwork.

Most of these so called "conversions" (not all) lack true repentance with fear and trembling, a firm understanding of the weight of the gospel, and a turning away from the world in order to follow Jesus. Most people today in churches may have experienced the Word, the excitement, or a touching sermon which allowed them to make a very quick emotional decision.

Jesus' ministry never looked like that. He actually said that it is possible to honor God with your lips, while your heart remains far from Him (Matthew 15:18). When people came to Jesus to follow Him, He was not so eager to just get people to make a quick rash decision. But He gave them hard realities at the onset of their interest in following Him. People would ask, "What will it take to follow you?"

He always replied the same thing: "It will take everything. It will cost you everything. Sell everything you have and give it to the poor. There is no time to say goodbye to your family. There is no time to bury your father. Let the dead bury the dead. You are coming to life! It is now or never. Think about it. Do not make a vow and break it. Count up the cost before you commit to this thing called the gospel!"

Do you see the extreme difference in how Jesus dealt with conversions versus what we commonly see today? We know Jesus is not actually requiring every Christian to sell all possessions nor requiring them to neglect honoring parents by giving them a nice send off. Instead, He told people who do not even know that He is the Son of God that they are having a conversation with God. And these people stop everything, drop their nets, leave their businesses, and follow Jesus.

This approach lets us know the level of commitment required in order to follow Jesus. One must hold Christ as so much more important than any of these carnal, temporal things. Some people would say, "Well, Jesus would never *actually* ask us that." That is not true. If you are listening and yielded, He just might ask you for a great sacrifice. The question is: *would you be willing to follow Jesus wherever He leads you?* Many people have been called by God to sell all of their possessions, to leave what was familiar and comfortable, and to go live on the streets on dirt roads in Africa to become missionaries.

Many have seen phenomenal fruit as a result of obeying God. Heidi and Rolland Baker are examples of that. They have highly affluent families, wealth, and doctoral degrees. And God told them to leave everything, sell their homes, and go become missionaries in Mozambique, Africa.

That command seemed to make no sense, and would be a hard word for anyone to follow, but they obeyed. Today, Heidi and Rolland Baker have walked in some of the greatest exploits seen or heard in this generation. They have seen over one million souls converted to the faith, discipled, and filled with the Spirit of God. They have seen over 500 raised from the dead, thousands of deaf ears opened, thousands of blinded eyes opened, and too many miracles to name or chronicle.

I could name a few examples of people who walk in that level of glory. It lets us know that Jesus' command to "do greater works" actually is possible and true. It is not for a select few. It is for anyone who believes in His name. The Bible uses a certain phrase over 20 times just before Jesus moved in healing and miracles: "and He was moved with compassion."

"And Jesus went forth, and saw a great multitude, and was moved with compassion toward them, and he healed their sick."
—**Matthew 14:14, KJV**

"Then Jesus called his disciples unto him, and said, 'I have compassion on the multitude, because they continue with me now three days, and have nothing to eat: and I will not send them away fasting, lest they faint in the way.'"
—**Matthew 15:32, KJV**

"Jesus had compassion on them and touched their eyes. Immediately they received their sight and followed him."
—Matthew 20:34, KJV

We have made such a big deal out of signs, miracles, and wonders, when Jesus said that signs, miracles, and wonder will naturally follow the life of a believer. Miracles are not out of the ordinary. They are not spectacular. They are not magnificent to the believer. The supernatural is as natural as breathing air in and out of your mouth.

Have you ever gotten excited about someone's breathing, who was otherwise healthy? No, because it is effortless. It is something that we do without even thinking about it. If someone is begging for money at a gate, we do not have to pray for ten hours. They do not even need to know a miracle is coming, or have faith for it. When we see someone's ailment, we too can be moved with compassion and just say "Take up your bed and walk" without breaking a sweat, without asking God if it is His will to give us what Jesus already settled at Calvary.

We can heal them and keep moving. Not just heal them without seeing the manifestation of the healing, either. There is a teaching that says your healing was purchased at Calvary 2,020 years ago, therefore you are already healed (present tense). We can send them away sick, confessing, "I am healed by the stripes of Jesus" as they are still completely ailing.

Wait one minute. Although that is doctrinally sound teaching and everything is true, we never one time see Jesus function like that. That is accommodating a lack of results. Don't get me wrong, that might be our experience (I've been there), but we don't shape our theology based off of our experiences, we shape our theology based upon the Word of God (which is Jesus).

Jesus, before Calvary, never sent anyone away sick who came to Him, sent for Him, or called out to Him. Neither did His twelve apostles. The one time the disciples tried and failed, they went to Jesus to learn why He could do it, and they couldn't. They didn't start making excuses, or creating new doctrines to reconcile why they didn't get results. They said to Jesus, "Why couldn't we do what you would have done had you been here!" (Matthew 17:19). And He told them!

We don't do that. We start trying to rationalize it when we see that we do not have such a good track record in healings or miracles. We start justifying our lack of results instead of pressing into God more and bringing our concerns to Jesus. Instead of going to God and saying, "Lord, you said we are as entitled to a healing as we are entitled to getting a sandwich to eat" (Matthew 16:26). "Lord, where is the disconnect? Why are we lacking what you said we could have?"

We have been hoodwinked and bamboozled by the devil. We are desensitized to the flow of God, going all the way back to Moses, Elijah, Elisha, and Abraham. Those patriarchs walked in exploits, talked with God, and understood Him regularly. Here we are, thousands of years later, with more than what they had. Our sin issue has been dealt with. We have been positionally made perfect. The veil has been torn. We have complete access to go before the throne of God. We are filled with the Holy Spirit and baptized with fire. We have more resources and tools (spiritually) than Moses, Elijah, Isaac, Abraham, or any of our biblical heroes ever had. Why then are we walking in far less glory and power?

    We are further along the timeline and we have less. Could you imagine what they would have done then if they had what we have now, by way of the Holy Spirit? We are so far removed from the flow of the Spirit, the supernatural, and the government of God.

    This wasn't so in the book of Acts. Remember that the saints were praying all night for Peter to be released from prison, and an angel went and broke him out of jail. Peter and the angel ran through the prison. The shackles just fell off and doors supernaturally opened. When Peter got back to the prayer meeting, where the Christians had been crying out to God for his release, Rhoda answered and said, "Peter is at the door!" (Acts 12:13).

    The church's reaction was like nothing we can relate to. They knew Peter was not dead, but they did not expect God to come through so quick. They told Rhoda, "It's not Peter. It must be his Angel!" They were so accustomed to the supernatural that it was easier for them to believe that an angel had showed up at their doorstep (looking like Peter), than for them to believe that Peter himself had been released. That literally means the supernatural was normal for them; they were accustomed to it.

Most Christians today would not believe it if they were told that an angel showed up at their doorstep. If one did, they would be scared out of their skin, and probably start questioning whether some sort of witchcraft was involved. Christians assign more power to Satan than God when it comes to the supernatural.

I remember one of the earliest miracles that I saw. I prayed for someone to conceive a child after failing to get pregnant and getting very discouraged about it. I saw and felt her pain, and I asked her if I could pray for her to conceive. She was shocked and surprised, although she was a Christian. I took her by the hand and spoke life to her womb.

The Holy Spirit spoke to me and said, "By this time next year, she will deliver a child." I told her exactly what the Spirit of the Lord said, and her eyes got really big and she started saying, "Don't play with me. This is a sensitive subject for me." But I knew what God had told me so I had zero skepticism. I didn't release that word and then start biting my nails saying, "God, please come through. Don't make me look bad." I told her, "When God says it, it's a done deal."

About 8 weeks later, I had a prophetic dream about her being pregnant. God even let me know that it would be a girl. I started calling her baby "Cinnamon." I would say "Cinnamon's on the way." She would just laugh and say, "I do want a girl, but whatever God blesses me with, I'll take."

Nine weeks from the release of that word, she conceived a girl whom she would name Vivian. She (my coworker) actually took the pregnancy test at work, and began to cry and rejoice and thank God. After the excitement ended and the smoke cleared, this Christian paused, and after two minutes, looked me in the eyes and said, "I have a serious question. Did you put some type of spell or witchcraft on me?"

My heart broke. The church is so desensitized to the power of God that it is easier for them to believe in demons than the supernatural power God. I told her, "No witchcraft, hex, or spell can do anything over the power of the Holy Spirit!"

When people see the gospel demonstrated, they are astonished and they glorify God. The bible says over 15 times that when Jesus healed someone, "they glorified God." So the supernatural always opened a door for ministry, and to show the love of God.

Jesus said, "Let your light so shine before men, that they might see your good works and glorify the Father in heaven." Love is not a good work or a spiritual gift. Love is not something that some believers have and others don't have. It is something we are all called to walk in. It is a foundation. Love is the essence and nature of a believer, because we are one with God, and God is love.

That being said, good works are actually things that involve an act of doing (healings, miracles, salvations, kind acts, etc.). So we must work out of love. It is the love of God that moves on our hearts and causes the supernatural to be released. Don't settle for kind gestures. Don't settle for the mundane. Don't settle for enticing words. Demonstrate the gospel every day of your life. That is our spiritual inheritance.

Our lives must look distinctly different from the world in every way. Just because you have a strong foundation does not mean that you stop building. If you need a place to live, you don't stop building the house just because the foundation is laid. You make sure your foundation is firm and built on the rock, and then you can create your mansion. Once your foundation is set, get ready to bring the kingdom of God into being through demonstrated power and love. Once you've built on the *rock* get ready to *shock*!

Fruitfulness is a key indicator to true discipleship in the mature believer. However, brokenness is a key cooperative component to fruitfulness. There is no fruitfulness without brokenness. In seeking God in our hearts, there must be a posture of repentance, seeking, yearning, and brokenness. Once our hearts are softened towards the Lord, we can hear Him and obey whatever He instructs us to do. I can prove it scripturally.

> *"I said, 'Plant the good seeds of righteousness, and you will harvest a crop of love. Plow up the hard ground of your hearts, for now is the time to seek the LORD, that he may come and shower righteousness upon you.'"*
> **—Hosea 10:12, KJV**

This verse is powerful because God is saying that we need to get busy working for Him and planting seeds, laboring so that we can reap a harvest. But the prerequisite to fruitfulness is always brokenness. He is saying to break up the fallow ground within your hearts; soften your hearts toward the Lord so that you can be used by Him, so that you can receive from Him.

Just like a farmer, if the ground is not plowed up or broken up, those seeds will not take root. They will not go into the earth. To get a large harvest there needs to be good, rich soil. This is an exact picture of what God needs from us! People of God, ready your hearts. When you are ready, the blessings and favor of God will begin to fall in your life like rain!

In Matthew chapter 13, Jesus told the parable of the sower. The sower cast his seeds onto four different types of ground: along the path, shallow ground, thorny ground, and good ground. These four types of soils represent the four conditions of the human heart. The seeds that fell along the path are those who hear the gospel, get emotionally charged, and make a decision that they didn't really understand. They don't last. The second type, the shallow ground, is a shallow heart. They receive the word, but there is no depth for the seed to burrow in and take root. The third type, the thorny ground, had some depth and the seed was rooted, but the weeds and thorns, representing life's worries and cares, become louder than the Word of God and eventually the plant is overpowered and dies.

But the fourth type, the good soil, is a heart that is broken before the Lord. It is someone who is so ready to receive what God is about to deposit in them. This heart has been well plowed. Before we met the Lord, we had been prepared through the Lord drawing us and dealing with us in our circumstances (really the devil was kicking our butts). We needed answers and were in search of something greater. Our hearts were ready. But once we get saved, that broken heart and tenderness must remain. This way we will be ready whenever God wants to deposit something within us. We will be ready to hear it, receive it, and give it out.

It is God who supplies seed to the sower. At one time we were the receivers, but the fruit in our life produced by a seed has now transitioned us to sower. As God gives to us, we give it away, and the cycle repeats. We are planting seeds of righteousness that will spring up into salvation. That means more than just getting people to heaven, but bringing heaven to earth.

So when we are sowing salvation into the earth, we are sowing healing, deliverance, and breakthrough. It is God who is the Lord of the breakthrough (2 Sam. 5:20). This lets us know how important brokenness is in bearing much fruit. A mature disciple understands this principle well.

Jesus was called the lion and the lamb. In prayer, we are so desperate for guidance, like lambs needing a shepherd. We yearn for Him, and our hearts melt. We understand our depravity in His presence. We know who we are and the grace that He has given us.

But when we go out to advance the kingdom, we should display the lion. It is time to move in power. We speak to the demons and tell them where to go. We cleanse all forms of sickness. We still the storms. We put all the power of the enemy under our feet.

Brokenness is God's pattern for extreme fruitfulness. It is His system of advancement. Jesus took the bread, He gave thanks, broke it, and then it multiplied (supernaturally). The extreme fruitfulness came after the brokenness.

> *"I tell you for certain that a grain of wheat that falls on the ground will never be more than one grain unless it dies. But if it dies, it will produce lots of wheat."*
> **—John 12:24, NIV**

Jesus, in speaking of His death and resurrection, gave a principle of brokenness. The seed itself cannot escape this spiritual law. The seed itself must die (become broken). It must lose its casing or shell for life to emerge from it. If it can go through that death process and become nothing—if it can embrace brokenness—fruitfulness will be the result. That very brokenness has the power to see an unlimited amount of grain produced in a crop of just one seed.

This is the exact image of what Jesus did when He died, and this is the charge that He has given His disciples. Like a seed, the heart has to become broken in order to produce. The bliss of heaven will never be ours until we break our bodies and shed our earth suits we call flesh. Until then, we will never emerge into eternity where we will experience boundless peace, joy, and love, and reign with God forever!

Look at the fruit that will come throughout the rest of eternity, yet everyone fears death. Jesus conquered death! There are no stings associated with death. Death is now a doorway to life! Embrace brokenness so that you can walk in fruitfulness!

8.
Are Tears Foolproof Access into Heaven?

> *"My sacrifice [the sacrifice acceptable] to God is a broken spirit; a broken and a contrite heart [broken down with sorrow for sin and humbly and thoroughly penitent], such, O God, You will not despise."*
> — **Psalm 51:17, *Amplified Bible, Classic Edition***

The scriptural references provided in this book are helpful to convey that our tears are important to God, and they connect us to the heart of God in a deep way. The message of this book is that weeping, tears, and contrition grab the attention of heaven, and will cause heaven to move swiftly on your behalf.

God delights when someone shows sincere repentance, deep sorrow, remorse, regret, and a genuine turning back to Him. It blesses God so much to see His children come to Him in humility and brokenness. He delights to move on your behalf.

With that being said, one may ask, "What if I don't cry? Can my prayers reach heaven and be effective and impactful?" I would respond, "yes," they technically could. However, when it comes to prayers of repentance or encountering God's presence, the tears will come without effort.

I recently prayed for someone who had no tear ducts. No matter how emotional she gets, no tears will be produced. She is also prone to eye infections and must self-lubricate her eyes daily. That is not how God created us to be. He created us to release tears for numerous reasons. We were not meant to hold onto our tears. We were designed to release them.

Crying reduces stress. Crying once a week can help reduce stress, according to a range of studies. One study—performed by Jonathan Rottenberg, Lauren M. Bylsma, and J.J.M. Vingerhoets—examined the effects of crying in 30 countries around the world. Crying was found to be a natural aid in reducing stress and building the immune system.[10]

Men are often conditioned that it is wrong or weak to cry. This is actually a lie of the enemy, which keeps men and church leaders physically sick, rather than emotionally healthy. This can have devastating effects; for example, pastors and church leaders have a high rate of suicide and heart attacks because they are under so much stress from the pressures of ministry.

My position is that it is okay to cry and release the stress; it is not a strike against masculinity. I am not advocating being an overly emotional man, crying and complaining about everything. What I am saying is that

---

[10] Jonathan Rottenberg, Lauren M. Bylsma, Ad J.J.M. Vingerhoets, "Is Crying Beneficial?" *Current Directions in Psychological Science* 17, no. 6 (Dec. 2008): 400-404.

when you feel legitimate pressure or stress, you have to let it out. If you don't let it out, it will find its own way out. It will come out in your temper, attitude, hair, body, and health.

My father pretty much trained me that real men do not cry. It was strongly implied, and I am sure that his father taught him that through word or deed. I have only seen him cry maybe twice in my life.

I initially gave my heart to Jesus at 9 years old. At sixteen, I wanted to really get serious about my walk, so I rededicated my life to the Lord. I told God that if He filled me with the Holy Spirit with the evidence of speaking in tongues, I would run for Him and never look back. While attending a revival, I remember asking my dad and mom about salvation. I said, "When I go to the altar and rededicate my heart to God, do I have to cry?"

"Yeah, you need to cry," my mom answered. "It is not a requirement, but it will just naturally happen when you're godly sorry. When you deeply repent and you're thankful for salvation, it'll just happen."

My dad replied, "No, you don't have to cry. But if you do that's cool. Some people cry, and some don't. If he doesn't cry, that doesn't mean he wasn't genuinely converted."

I appreciated my dad's statement. It's true in theory. I really did not believe that I had any tears in me to release. I just wanted to be saved. I didn't think all the extra stuff was necessary. I wasn't against it, but I knew that I wanted more of God. I didn't want people to feel I was not sincere because there were no tears.

     Leading up to the night of the revival, I had been fasting with no food or water, reading my Bible daily, watching no television, and listening to no secular music. The night had come and I gave my heart to the Lord in the meeting. I repented and I did not cry! I felt really good; I meant it from my heart, but no tears came. I didn't feel bad at all. I knew that I was sincere.

     I remember at the end of the service, I went and hugged my mom. She said, "I'm glad you gave your heart to God."

     "I'm glad to be saved," I said. She embraced me and we hugged. Then, out of nowhere, I started weeping unexpectedly with such gratitude and thanksgiving for Jesus saving me. That was actually the first time that I felt the Spirit of God. I just didn't have a paradigm for it at the time.

     After I released my mom, she told me, "The Spirit of God is on you. Had you kept going, you could have been filled with the baptism of the Holy Ghost all in one night." Two nights later, I was filled with the Holy Spirit and I never looked back. That was 16 years ago.

     As a disclaimer, I will say that tears are not foolproof access into heaven. Some people are naturally more emotional, and they cry about everything; or they are more apt to cry even if they do not hit their deepest place of emotion. For example, women are naturally more emotional, and it is easier for them to get to that place of tears than most men.

The Bible actually says, "Call for the wailing women to come" (Jeremiah 9:17, NIV). According to Ellicott's Commentary,

> Eastern funerals were, and are, attended by mourners, primarily women, hired for the purpose of crying. Wailing was reduced to an art, and they who practiced it were cunning. There are the "mourners" that "go about the streets" (Ecclesiastes 12:5), those that "are skillful of lamentation" (Amos 5:16).[11]

It appears that these women were actually able to cry on command, and had it down to a science. Even though wailing and mourning can be doctrinally sound and effective, it is possible to take something good and manipulate it so that it loses its intended value.

Both of my kids, Khloe and Jackson, would cry when they were babies and they needed something. I would immediately drop what I was doing and run to tend to their needs. Once they began to understand that daddy comes quickly when I cry, they started making themselves cry on purpose. The tears began to lose their value, and I had to discern the tone of the cry in order to tell if it was sincere or not.

Likewise, God is a discerner of the thoughts and intentions of the heart (Hebrews 4:12). You cannot

---

[11] Charles Ellicott, commentary on Jeremiah 9:17, in *Ellicott's Commentary for English Readers*, (London: Cassell and Company, 1897).

manipulate God with insincere crying. I am not saying that if you are not bringing some water out of your eyes that God will never hear you. I am simply giving you some principles that are keys to touch heaven and will help to deploy the hand of God in your life.

A few years ago, I visited what I thought was a ministry, but was actually a cult. The leader cried every time he would sing a song. Judging from the outside, you would immediately think, "Man, this guy knows the Lord." I have never seen a man or woman cry so dramatically and so (seemingly) sincerely. He would sing these songs out of his heart, and he would cry so profusely that it was almost mesmerizing and captivating. It made me think, "Wow, I've cried out of my heart, but never like that."

After a few months, God gave me a vision about this cult leader that was very bad. I kept the vision from my wife because I wanted to stay around the ministry, because I thought it was powerful and I wanted more of God. Three weeks later, my wife had a dream that this leader was sexually inappropriate with the women in the ministry. It went beyond a weakness or just messing up; it was demonic and predatory. After we shared our words from the Lord, we never went back.

I began researching that cult, and that leader had been preying on the body of Christ for over 30 years—sleeping with women and men, molesting children, beating his workers, depriving them of food and pay, and more. His ex-wife released a video stating that when the two were married, documented evidence surfaced that he slept with over 40 women at one time; slept with all 8 deacons' wives; got three women pregnant; and forced one woman to abort their child. The same year that we left, over 100 women came forward saying that they had also been sexually active with him, including a prominent gospel singer.

The point is that looks can be deceiving. As Scripture says, "Man looks on the outward appearance, but God looks on the heart" (1 Sam. 16:7). This minister's heart could not have been further away from the heart of Jesus, but judging from his weeping and mourning, one might easily conclude that he was the real deal.

Brokenness is a key attribute to touching the heart of God, but the true measure is that your heart is transformed and you begin to look like God, act like God, walk like God, and talk like God. You should be conformed daily to the image of Jesus.

As we have seen, tears are not foolproof access to God. Sincere tears are an indication that we are close to God's heart and presence. Brokenness, contrition, and a repentant heart attract the presence of God into your life. When we humble ourselves in prayer, humility, and meekness, God's presence will overtake you so fast it will make your head spin.

This was demonstrated memorably in Scripture when God spared the wicked king Ahab because of his brokenness. Ahab was the most evil ruler of Israel. Because of the evil he did as king, God sentenced him to disaster, ruin, and death. But when Ahab heard of God's judgment, he fell on his face before the Lord and pleaded for mercy.

> *"Have you noticed how Ahab has humbled himself before me? Because he has humbled himself, I will not bring this disaster in his day, but I will bring it on his house in the days of his son."*
> **—1 Kings 21:29**

Notice how Ahab turned from cheating and lying to humility and repentance. He asked for mercy out of his heart, and God quickly revoked the judgment. If brokenness and repentance works for the most wicked king, how much more will God look favorably upon His own children that humble themselves in true repentance and brokenness before Him! Indeed, "God opposes the proud, but gives grace to the humble" (James 4:6; 1 Peter 5:5). As Nicole Kauffman observed,

> God makes countless promises to the humble throughout Scripture. Humility is a big deal to God. Countless times throughout Scripture, God gave mercy to those who humbled themselves before Him.[12]

Remember, not all tears awaken our Lord's compassion. God has little patience when we weep in misery over the idols that He removes from us. He does not grant blessings when we profusely weep, but lack a repentant heart, as occurred when Israel preferred Egypt's meat to God's presence (Numbers 11:4-10).

---

[12] Nicole Kauffman, "7 Promises God Makes to the Humble," *Courage Hope Love* (blog), last modified February 6, 2017, https://couragehopelove.com/promises-to-the-humble/.

For those who possess a repentant heart, every tear that you shed in faith has this banner hanging over it: "The Lord is near to the brokenhearted" (Psalms 24:18).

9.

The Tear Room in Heaven

"You keep track of all my sorrows. You have collected all my tears in your bottle. You have recorded each one in your book."
— **Psalms 56:8, NLT**

I never had any intention of writing a book. One day, as I was in prayer and meditating on God's Word, it was as if this book was *downloaded* to my spirit. When I came out of prayer, I knew that I was supposed to write this book. I knew every chapter, the teachings, and the revelations. I had never even heard of a "tear room" or read about anyone visiting one. However, I knew that one of the chapters in my book was to be called "The Tear Room in Heaven"!

I began to inquire of the Lord about the tear room, and what He would have us know about this room. He immediately took me took me to Psalm 56:8 (NLT): "You keep track of all my sorrows. You have collected all my tears in your bottle. You have recorded each one in your book."

I may have previously skimmed over that verse in passing, but I had never given it any significant thought. This verse was now the confirmation that I needed to validate this room in heaven. I asked God to grant me the grace to have a visitation or an encounter in this room, so that I may write by experience. For several months, I worked tirelessly on this book. I had to skip this chapter because God had as of yet not granted me the encounter in the tear room. I completed the entire book and the night I finished the book, I had an encounter in the tear room.

As I meditated on Psalm 56:8, I imagined worshipping God before His throne, as I was quoting this passage. It is important to engage our own imaginations when we are praying and worshiping. However, never allow your imagination to run wild. While praying in tongues, when the Bible says your mind is unfruitful (1 Cor. 14:14), it refers only to the frontal lobe of the brain which is responsible for language. Other components of the brain remain active, like our imagination. If we do not tame it, it will begin to run wild.

Often times while praying in tongues, you will begin to see mental images of things that you need to do, unrelated to God. You may see yourself taking care of the kids, watching television, cooking dinner, going to work, or talking to your spouse. These are all distractions to that moment of consecration. Most of the time, those distractions are not the enemy; they are just the way we are wired. We were created with an imagination. God gave us the imagination, and that is how we connect to Him.

> *In the last days, God says, I will pour out My Spirit on all people… your young men will see visions, your old men will dream dreams.*
> —**Acts 2:17, NIV**

As Scripture says, in the last days, the language of the Holy Spirit will be dreams and visions. Dreams and visions are a component of our imagination. This is why so many people say, "God deals with me in my dreams," because that restful state is when your soul is quieted and God can get through to you. The point is that when we are seeking God in any capacity, capture your thoughts and use your imagination to engage God. You do not have to wait for Him to come and fall on you. No, pursue Him! By faith *you* may "go boldly to His throne of grace that you might obtain grace and mercy in your time of need" (Hebrews 4:16)!

As I meditated on Psalm 56, I opened my heart and worshiped the Lord. I imagined being before His throne as I was speaking the Word of God in Psalm 56. After about 30 minutes of letting that verse saturate my soul, I went into an encounter! Jesus walked up to me and said that He wanted to show me something. I stood up and began following Him down a corridor. We went into this huge room that was very upscale! It had gold, crystal, diamonds, and chandeliers.

As we walked deeper into the room, I noticed countless shelves holding bottles filled with what I knew were tears! These bottles were shaped like tears—basically like a Hershey's kiss. They were made in all different sizes, each assigned to a unique person. It seemed as though the size of each bottle was pre-determined to hold the capacity of tears that its owner would cry on earth.

As we continued to walk through the tear room, I became more fascinated with the tear bottles, as if I were a kid in a candy store. Jesus knew my excitement, smiled, and slowed down for me, so that I might tour the room. As I got closer, I saw that each bottle had different designs, decorations, and stones in them. Some were trimmed in diamonds, and the owner's name was engraved in gold. I saw Moses's tear bottle. I saw Elijah's tear bottle. I noticed as I got closer, that the tears were still crying out—I could actually hear the sounds of the individuals as their tears were created.

From there, I saw more of the older saints and patriarchs. As I continued on, I saw the bottle of Kathryn Kuhlman! She was always one of my favorite generals. As I began to focus on her tears, I could not only hear her crying, but I could see visual images of her timeline on earth and how these tears were created. It was so amazing to see some of her personal moments with the Lord.

Kuhlman had such a tender heart towards the Lord, and she was so full of passion. In my assessment of what I watched, she really took an unhealthy burden for things that happened in her ministry that were beyond her control or responsibility. Even in her highest and most notable moments on earth, she always had brokenness behind the scenes. It goes beyond what most will ever know.

As the Lord and I continued to walk, there was a section in the room full of angels that were sitting and writing. These were the scribe angels whose sole responsibility was recording and chronicling the events that caused God's children to weep.

The angels were so detailed. Not only were they writing what happened, but they were numbering the events! There was a circular contraption in the middle of a room that reminded me of a well. As I got closer to it, I saw the entire universe, and planet earth looked like a small tennis ball. It was beyond HD or 4K.

I saw angels ascending and descending through what I now know was a portal. These angels were going to retrieve the tears from earth and bring them back to heaven. Jesus switched the scene to show me how the process worked. I saw an angel collecting the tears of a single mom struggling with her children. She was unemployed and had a sick child. She was completely burnt out in life and wanted to give up. Not only was this angel collecting her tears, but he also was sent to give her supernatural strength!

Many times when we are distressed, angels are sent to minister to us and strengthen us, although we do not see them. Sometimes we just say, "I feel the presence of the Lord." This woman felt God's presence without noticing the angel. She took a deep breath, let out a sigh of relief, and stopped crying. This was the angel strengthening her. After she felt stronger, the angel came back to heaven through the portal. I was blown away!

We continued to walk through this room and I looked at more tear bottles. Then I came across Jesus's bottle. I was shocked at the size of it. It appeared to me to have been a couple of gallons, which was big compared to the average bottle. I was shocked, because I knew that He only lived until 33 years old. It seemed as though He shed a lot of tears in a short period of time. As I gazed into the tears, I saw segments of Jesus's life and His burden and love for humanity. Jesus truly has a love that is unfathomable, and a supreme love for His Father.

His most intense prayer was in the garden before His crucifixion. However, all of His prayers were intense and full of passion. I saw Him frequently crying when He approached His Father in prayer. Jesus embodied humility and reliance on the Father. He epitomized having a heart of brokenness and contrition. As I saw His scenes play out, I wept. It was not easy to see my contribution to His plight and to witness the love that He demonstrated towards me.

I went up to Jesus, hugged Him, and cried on His white robe. He comforted me and began to cry with me. It was an amazing moment. I saw His tear bottle self-generating tears while He was crying on my shoulder. Even the tears that we both cried in heaven were not wasted!

We walked even further. I would guess that we only covered about 2 percent of the contents of the tear room! As I walked further down, I was shocked by the next two bottles. I saw bottles of tears for Ramesses and Adolf Hitler! I was immediately confused. I looked to Jesus, and was wondering why their tears were here, but my lips never moved.

He telepathically answered me (spirit-to-spirit) and said, "They're all loved the same!" I was blown away. I would have never thought that these people's tears were in heaven!

"Wait one minute, Jesus!" I responded. "You're telling me that Moses, Elijah, Kathryn Kuhlman, and Adolf Hitler all share a space in the same room?! And the Father's love for Kathryn Kuhlman is no different than His love for Ramesses?

Jesus answered, "It's all the same."

I was shocked that God's love remains constant even for the most wicked people imaginable. It is not God's will for any human on earth to die and go to hell. No matter how bad you are, His arms are always open. He cares for you and loves you in a way that will always remain steadfast and unconditional! Even though not everyone will make it to heaven, each person still has things in heaven that belong to them, because God makes preparations in heaven for all of us!

I saw God in this room. It was almost like a sentimental room of reflection and contemplation. It is so amazing how God shows love and emotions like humans; this truly conveyed that we are made in His image and likeness!

My wife and I lost our first son, Jonathan, when he was only 19 weeks old, and we have a memory box for him. It contains his blanket, his hat, and other sentimental artifacts that remind us of that moment in time seven years ago. The blanket and hat even have his scent, and some of his bodily fluids are stained on the garments. Every now and then we will go in that room and look through his box, smell his garments, and think about our dear son. Even though we lost him, he still holds a special place in our hearts.

This is exactly how God views the tear room. He goes in and reminisces about those precious moments of His children. Even though He may have lost some of them, they are no less dear to Him. The love of God is truly indescribable!

God loves His children with a wild, passionate, obsessive love (yes, *obsessive*). He will never stop loving you! If you can count the grains of sand on the ocean banks, then you can count the Father's thoughts towards you (Psalm 139:17-18). He has assigned each hair on your head a number (Matthew 10:30). He has bottled up every tear that you have ever cried!

In the tear room of heaven, every deed of righteousness is immortalized! Everything is chronicled faithfully in heaven—every temptation resisted; every evil overcome; every word of pity; every heartfelt prayer! Every sacrifice, suffering, and sorrow endured for Christ's sake is recorded in His book!

10.
Tears Will Cease

"He will wipe away every tear from their eyes, and death shall be no more, neither shall there be mourning, nor crying, nor pain anymore, for the former things have passed away." And he who was seated on the throne said, "Behold, I am making all things new."
—**Revelation 21:4-5, ESV**

Many of us feel ashamed of our tears, especially if others see them. In a culture that prizes strength, many of us respond to our own tears with a hasty wipe of the sleeve. We have adopted the "get over it" mentality.

This is not the case with Daddy God, who has the love of a tender Father. His compassion compels Him to draw near to the brokenhearted and bind up their wounds (Psalm 147:3). The God who said "Blessed are you who weep now" (Luke 6:21) will not reproach you for the tears you shed while you walk through our broken world.

God fully understands what we go through on earth as His children. He has a plan to remove the pain, sorrow, and weeping that we experience on earth. The Bible says that "weeping may endure for a night, but joy comes in the morning" (Psalm 30:5). When they lay us to rest in the earth, we will wake up in paradise in the presence of Jehovah. One of God's promises to us is the fullness of everlasting joy (Psalm 16:11).

Down here on earth, tears are a natural part of the human language. It is a part of emotion. It is a natural response when we hit a certain threshold of pain, pleasure, or joy. It is a part of the response that our bodies produce when we are afflicted in body or soul. Tears become a part of the way we earnestly contend for the faith.

Repentance should be a part of the daily regime of the believer. I repent every single day, throughout the day, even when there is no conscious sin of which I am aware. I repent all the time, because I really want to stay close to the heart of God and in close fellowship with Him. However, a day is coming when the need to contend for the faith will be over. Weeping and mourning will cease. In heaven, there will be no need for tears. Jesus calls it paradise; it will far exceed our hopes or dreams.

My wife and I love to travel. We have been blessed to go a few places that were pretty nice. I really liked going to Jamaica and Hawaii. To me, Hawaii was the one place I thought would be a vacation I enjoyed the most. We stayed at an island called Moloka'i, and we also went to Maui.

These islands were beautiful, and so peaceful! Our resort was rated at five stars, and was directly on the ocean. When we sat on the shore, watching the sunset and listening to the waves, I thought about how God is so amazing. "What a great way to get away from the cares of life," I said. "What's better than this?"

A couple of years later, we were blessed to go on a vacation to Puerto Vallarta, Mexico. The resort we stayed at was really nice—unlike anything you've ever seen. Many celebrities stay there, such as Shakira, Justin Bieber, Tiger Woods, and more.

"Is this a five star resort?" I asked.

The travel expert almost laughed, and said, "No, it is much higher than that. This exceeds the star ratings of normal hotels. *Diamonds* are the next level of rating."

I had never heard of rooms costing $7,000 per night (thank God we did not have to pay that!). She explained the diamond scale to me. One diamond is higher than five stars. Our resort was *five diamonds*!

I was shocked. This resort was unlike anything we had ever seen or experienced in our life. I didn't know what could have topped Hawaii, but this was it. We were like two kids in a candy store. Hawaii was *amazing* but this resort made Moloka'i look like the projects. I told my wife, "This is literally heaven on earth."

It looked like someone had cut each blade of grass, one by one, and painted them each vibrant green. All of the mulch was perfectly in place. The water was crystal clear in every river, every water fall, and even the ocean. Nothing was faded. Nothing was missing. Nothing was broken.

The customer service exceeded Disney world. The attendants catered to us hand and foot. They went the extra mile in everything they did. When we would walk into a room, they would light up and smile like we were celebrities. They would put their right hand over their hearts and bow. I thought, "These people are brainwashed. How do you get a whole resort to act this happy and attentive every day?"

The food was diamond level. There was a breakfast buffet that was *so good*! Most buffets are nasty: the kids play in the food, the food gets old and cold, messes are spilled, everything is germy, and the actual quality of the food is low. At this resort, however, the buffet was at the level of Ruth Chris Steak House—but you could eat all that you wanted.

Everything tasted like it was made from the highest quality gourmet ingredients. The presentation was unparalleled. The décor was heavenly. The room had skyscraper ceilings. There were over 200 food items and 15 different flavors of freshly squeezed juices.

As I fixed my plate, my hands literally shook and my eyes bulged. I was like a drug addict with mouth watering. I said to my wife, "Honey, surely the Lord is in this place. This is *Bethel*!"

My wife was looking at me like I was insane, as she often does. The waiter came and asked about our meal. I said, "This is the greatest experience of my life! The food is absolutely amazing! I believe there literally are angels in the kitchen preparing this food!"

The waitress laughed out loud, and said, "I'm glad you guys are enjoying it." She backed away slowly and cautiously.

That experience in Mexico did not solve any of our problems, financial burdens, or stressors back home. But for that week of paradise, it seemed as if we didn't have a care in the world. It was a euphoric experience. The weight of the beauty, splendor, and perfection overwhelmed any thought of negativity of what would be waiting for us back home.

In Romans 8:18, Apostle Paul writes, "I am convinced that any suffering we endure is less than nothing compared to the magnitude of glory that is about to be unveiled." In the same way, our trip to Mexico wiped away the memory and stress of life back home—at least for a moment. Heaven's beauty will far exceed any pain or sorrow that we ever faced on earth.

There are places on earth much nicer than the Grand Mayan Resort in Puerto Vallarta. But even if you get the nicest, most elaborate getaway location on earth, it will seem equivalent to the projects or the worst ghetto in comparison to heaven. The weight of glory in heaven is so extravagant that it will completely obliterate the pain of anything negative we experienced on earth! Our sorrow, tears, and disappointments will not even be worthy to be mentioned.

There is coming a time when God will remove all tears from His redeemed ones. "He will swallow up death forever. The Sovereign LORD will wipe away the tears from all faces; He will remove his people's disgrace from all the earth" (Isaiah 25:8). The apostle John quotes Isaiah's prophecy as he records his vision of heaven in Revelation 7:17. At the very end of time, God fulfills

His promise: "He will wipe every tear from their eyes" (Revelation 21:4).

11.
Jesus Empathizes With Your Tears

"For Jesus is not some high priest who has no sympathy for our weaknesses and flaws. *He has already been tested in every way that we are tested; but He emerged victorious, without failing God."*
— **Hebrews 4:15,** *The Voice*

As we learn in this verse, Christ was tempted in every possible way—there was no condition or ailment of humanity that He did not face through temptation and overcome. This passage really emphasizes that Jesus possessed humanity and divinity at the same time. He did not come and redeem mankind as God, but He redeemed it as a man completely reliant on the Holy Spirit.

Jesus showed us the path that we are to take in this life, and He showed us how to live victoriously. In other words, while Jesus was on earth, it was not easy for Him. He was a man: He got tired; He slept; He ate; He went to the bathroom; He cooked and barbecued (John 21:9-10). He battled against the enemy's temptation and He bled. Jesus knows what we are dealing with: loneliness, rejection, neglect, and depression. He sympathizes and empathizes with every tear that we shed.

His care for humanity is displayed countless times, as Scripture recounts his earthly ministry.

> *"When Jesus caught sight of the city, he burst into tears with uncontrollable weeping over Jerusalem, saying, "If only you could recognize that this day peace is within your reach! But you cannot see it."*
> — **Luke 19:41-42, *The Passion Translation***

When Jesus joined a crowd outside the town of Nain, He watched a widow weep over her son's body and "He had compassion on her" (Luke 7:13). Other times, when Jesus was about to perform a miracle, it was preceded with His compassion. It was His empathy for the condition of the individual that drove Him to action.

I believe we will see an increase of miracles, healings, and signs when our hearts begin to shift from our own ministry, churches, and branding towards a heart for humanity. Godliness has nothing to do with building anything of my own, nothing to do with showcasing my gifts. But when I see a single mother struggling to pay the bills for her 3-year-old son with leukemia, I am moved with compassion. I am setting the table for the supernatural power of God to intervene. This is bringing the kingdom into being.

Jesus was not only moved with compassion; He would get in the ring with the victims and start crying with them. The amazing thing was that He knew that He was about to fix everything! Jesus was truly man, through and through. His heart is so connected to the wellbeing of humanity that He literally cries with creation in its adversity. Later, when Mary fell apart at Jesus's feet over the death of her brother, the Scriptures say that "Jesus wept" (John 11:35).

Jesus wept with compassion—even though He was about to speak the word to snatch them both back from death (Luke 7:14; John 11:43). Just because Jesus loves us and has the power to fix our problems, does not mean that He takes a shortcut through our grief. The same one who raises the dead first stops to linger with us in our sorrow, in order to let us know that He sees what we are going through and that He cares.

Jesus faced some trials that are unfathomable. I could not imagine the depth of prayer He needed to carry the weight of humanity on His shoulders. When Jesus was in the garden, praying to God before He was offered up to be crucified, He cried loudly and vehemently; He screamed, groaned, and wept sorely. We know that it was severe because blood started seeping through His pores. This would have been a sight to see.

Although there is much to unpack here, it is clear to see His humanity through it all. Jesus did not want to die. He knew in His heart that everything He came to do led up to that moment, yet He pleaded with God. Screaming to the top of His lungs, He prayed, "Dad, if there is any possible way please let this bitter cup pass! Dad, what's the other alternative? Dad, what is Plan B?" This was far worse than He could have anticipated.

Some people might think, "Well, if I was on death row, I would have been screaming and crying too." Not necessarily. Plenty have died a gruesome death on death row and had peace with it, accepting it for what it was. We see this with Peter, who the night before he was to be executed, fell asleep between two soldiers (Acts 12:6).

Jesus was vexed in His soul because He knew the key to effective prayer and capturing the heart of God! He knew the power of humbling himself before God. He knew the power of brokenness. He knew the power of contrition and being poor in spirit. He needed His Father to move swiftly on His behalf. He lay before His Father in the garden and poured out His soul like Hannah, Hezekiah, Nehemiah, and so many others.

> *"While he lived on earth, anticipating death, Jesus offered up both [specific] petitions and [urgent] supplications [for that which He needed] with strong crying and vehement tears to the One who was [always] able to save Him from death, and He was heard because of His reverent submission toward God. Though he was God's Son, he learned trusting-obedience by what he suffered, just as we do. Then, having arrived at the full stature of his maturity and having been announced by God as high priest in the order of Melchizedek, he became the source of eternal salvation to all who believingly obey him."*
> —**Hebrews 5:7-10,** ***The Message***

Jesus empathized with so many others who faced turmoil and agony, but here He faced His giant; He faced the cross. He prayed; He petitioned; He wept; He travailed for a breakthrough and He got one!

Some might ask, "How did He get a breakthrough if God didn't remove the cup and He still died?" In fact, God did come through for Jesus, because He released a grace and a supernatural strength to His Son. It could have only been imparted to Him through prayer, allowing Him to be able to endure this horrible death by crucifixion. Here is Jesus's prayer:

> *"Father, if You are willing, take this cup from Me. Yet not My will, but Yours be done." And there appeared an angel unto him from heaven, strengthening him.*
> **—Luke 22:42-43**

God literally released an angel from heaven for Jesus. The angel injected strength into Jesus physically, mentally, and emotionally so that He could successfully accomplish His purpose! (This is what I saw in the tear room!)

Jesus's execution was much worse than what most criminals faced for their crimes. First, the whipping that Jesus endured was more severe, to the degree that if you saw Him afterward, you would barely be able to tell that He was human (Isaiah 52:14). Second, Jesus endured the mental and emotional pain of abandonment—becoming forsaken by God and the literal scapegoat for sinners.

> *"You are My Son; today I have become Your Father."*
> **—Hebrews 5:5, NIV**
> *"Although he was a son, he learned obedience from what he suffered and, once made perfect, he became the source of eternal salvation for all who*

> *obey him and was designated by God to be high priest in the order of Melchizedek."*
> **—Hebrews 5:8-10, NIV**

Jesus battled negative thoughts and overcame them by the Spirit. It was His thoughts of humanity coming to salvation—including you, personally—which gave Him joy and supernatural strength to endure the cross! Jesus weeping before the Lord set the table for an eternal harvest of souls. Although He was a Son, He learned obedience from what He suffered, and basically was promoted to another level of sonship and authority that He would have never known aside from this experience.

The Scriptures often tell us that we reap what we sow, but there is one particular verse that is an anomaly to that law of sowing and reaping. It is a powerful prayer principle as well:

> *"They that sow in tears shall reap in joy."*
> **—Psalms 126:5, KJV**

Nothing can capture the heart of God like a humble servant, broken and contrite before Him. God will never reject that servant or turn him away. We might think, "If we sow in tears, then we will reap in tears."

But that's not right. If we sow in tears and continue to pursue the face of God, we will eventually inherit a harvest that will speak on our behalf throughout eternity. This is Jesus's testimony, and He came down to show us that if He could do it, then we could do it. He was the first fruit of many brethren.

As Scott Hubbard noted, tears and sorrow have a sanctifying effect on the Christian which prepares us in anticipation for reunion with the Lord:

> Every tear that you shed is preparing for you "an eternal weight of glory beyond all comparison" (2 Corinthians 4:17). Every drop of agony and heartache sinks down into the ground like a seed, waiting to sprout up into an oak of laughter.
>
> Maybe that sounds impossible. Maybe you wonder, "How could *this* sorrow, *this* heartache, *this* grief ever give way to joy?" That's alright if you can't understand the how right now. God's ways are often too high and too marvelous for us to grasp. But can you believe — in hope against hope — that what is impossible with man is possible with God (Luke 18:27; Romans 4:18).
>
> Believing that God will turn our tears into shouts of joy does not mean that we no longer grieve. But it does mean that we cling to him through the pain, and let every calamity crash us into his arms. And that we learn to lament to God instead of curse his name.
>
> We'll keep reading our Bibles, even when we feel dead to God's word. We'll keep on crying out to God, even when he feels deaf to us. We'll keep on gathering with God's people, even when they don't understand what we're going through. We'll keep on serving others, even while we carry our sorrow wherever we go. And we'll keep on sowing the seeds of truth and grace into our barren

souls, waiting for the day when God takes us home.[13]

When He takes us home, God will wipe away every tear from our eyes and we reign with Him in everlasting joy forever.

---

[13] Scott Hubbard, "What God Says to Your Tears," *Desiring God*, last modified March 8 2018, https://www.desiringgod.org/articles/what-god-says-to-your-tears.

Conclusion

As we have covered in the preceding chapters, tears have a role to play in the life of a Christian believer. Many biblical figures, including the prophet Jeremiah, the apostle Paul, and even the Lord Jesus Christ, experienced incidents during their respective ministries that moved them to weeping. We may acknowledge that, in the right context, even the strongest and godliest of people may cry, including the flawless God-man Himself.

We have noted that tears are meaningful only within certain parameters, namely, when accompanied by true Christian faith and heartfelt sincerity. If either of these factors are lacking, then tears will lose their heavenly appeal. No amount of tears will make up for a lack of faith in Christ; in fact, there will be endless weeping in Hell (Matthew 8:12). Furthermore, God will not be fooled by insincere crying. The Lord cannot be manipulated with a self-induced emotional display. It would be both wrong and ineffective to generate tears as a means of appealing to God in prayer.

Sincere tears are a byproduct of one's internal brokenness, a virtue as taught by Jesus when He said, "Blessed are the poor in spirit" and "Blessed are those who mourn" (Matthew 5:3, 4). The Lord looks with compassion on those who are genuinely broken over something relevant to the faith. In the first place, God expects His people to be sincerely repentant and remorseful over their sinfulness. It would not be too much to say that a believer ought to be broken about their own sin to the point of tears. Second, God is tender towards those who petition Him for a holy cause with a broken heart. Third, God is compassionate when His children are broken because of suffering.

Another context in which tears are prevalent is in Christian ministry. When Apostle Paul gave his farewell address to the Ephesian elders (Acts 20), he recounted that he lived among them for years "serving the Lord with all humility and with tears" (v. 19). His tears seemed to be relevant to the great urgency he felt in delivering the message of the gospel to the community and to protecting the flock of believers entrusted to him. He warned them to "be alert, remembering that for three years I did not cease to admonish everyone with tears" (v. 31). Finally, his speech ended with "much weeping on the part of all" (v. 37). Ministers and laypeople alike ought to use Paul's urgency and seriousness as a model for their own evangelism and role within the church.

While tears clearly have a role to play in the life of a believer, there will come a time when their tears will cease. When the saints are resurrected and brought to the Father's house, there will be no more brokenness, hurt, or remorse—only joy. The Lord "wipes away every tear from their eyes" (Rev. 7:17). By this we may observe then that while tears are not necessarily sinful, they are only generated because of the pains induced by the presence of sin. In the holy perfection of heaven, there will be "no more crying" (Rev. 21:4).

Nonetheless, the saints will continuously be afflicted by the effects of sin during their earthly lives.

While running the race of faith, it would be quite normal for one to be moved to tears over the struggles and challenges faced in the world. This survey of biblical examples has not only proven that it is no shame to cry, but has encouraged believers to be expressive with their emotions when it is appropriate. Christians have no reason be stoic or reserved to the point where they suppress all tears within the family of God.

      Finally, let us interpret this entire work within the framework of the Christian gospel, the rock foundation upon which we stand. The good news that was delivered to humanity is the revelation that God sent His own divine Son to save a remnant from the Lord's coming wrath due to sin. Jesus, the prophesied Messiah and Savior, was born of a virgin, lived a sinless life, and then died a vicarious death in the place of every one who would ever believe in Him. His death was a sacrifice and propitiation to God the Father, and it was offered and accepted once for all time for the forgiveness of sins. This saving message is now preached to the world, and eternal life is promised to all those who hear this gospel and believe that the Lord Jesus died in their place and rose from the tomb. It is to God's glory that we now exercise faith and live in obedience to Him awaiting the time when tears will be turned to joy. Amen.

Bibliography

Andrew, Steven. "Heal Our Land and Lives by One Year of National Repentance." *USA Christian Church* (blog). Last modified 2017. https://www.usa.church/two-months-national-repentance-2/.

Campisi, Tom. "Did David Wilkerson Give a Prophecy About a Plague in New York City Back in 1986?" *Tri-State Voice* (blog). Last modified April 10, 2020. https://tristatevoice.com/2020/04/10/did-david-wilkerson-give-a-prophecy-about-a-plague-in-new-york-city-back-in-1986/.

"Crying Once a Week Can Reduce Stress – Says Japanese 'Tears teacher.' *Not Salmon* (blog). Accessed May 2, 2020. www.notsalmon.com/2018/10/26/crying-reduce-stress/.

Ellicott, Charles. *Ellicott's Commentary for English Readers.* London: Cassell and Company, 1897.

Gayle, Rhoda. "Bob Jones' Viral Prophecy Claims The Kansas City Chiefs Win Is A Sign Of Revival Coming." *God TV* (blog). Last modified February 3, 2020. https://godtv.com/bob-jones-prophecy-kansas-city-chiefs/.

Gendry, Sebastian. "Why It Is Important to Embrace Your Tears." *Laughter Online University* (blog). Accessed May 7, 2020. https://www.laughteronlineuniversity.com/importance-of-tears/.

Hubbard, Scott. "What God Says to Your Tears." *Desiring God.* Last modified March 8, 2018. https://www.desiringgod.org/articles/what-god-says-to-your-tears.

Kauffman, Nicole. "7 Promises God Makes to the Humble." *Courage Hope Love* (blog). Last modified February 6, 2017. https://couragehopelove.com/promises-to-the-humble/.

"Maria Woodworth-Etter: Grandmother of the Pentecostal Movement," Believers Portal (blog), last modified February 8, 2019, https://believersportal.com/maria-woodworth-etter-grandmother-of-the-pentecostal-movement/.

Orloff, Judith. "The Health Benefit of Tears," *Psychology Today.* Last modified July 27, 2010.

https://www.psychologytoday.com/us/blog/emotional-freedom/201007/the-health-benefits-tears.

Rottenberg, Jonathan, Lauren M. Bylsma, and Ad J.J.M. Vingerhoets. "Is Crying Beneficial?" *Current Directions in Psychological Science* 17, no. 6 (Dec. 2008): 400-404.

Sharma, Pooja. "Why Do We Cry? The Science of Tears." *Healthy Hub* (blog). Last modified July 30, 2018. https://healthyhub.org/why-do-we-cry-the-science-of-tears/.

"Smith Wigglesworth's 1939 Prophesy." *Call The Nation To Prayer* (blog). Last modified December 29, 2018. https://ctntp.uk/2018/12/29/smith-wigglesworths-1939-prophecy/.

"What does it mean to work out salvation with fear and trembling (Philippians 2:12)?" *Got Questions Ministries*. Accessed May 1, 2020. https://www.gotquestions.org/fear-and-trembling.html.

Made in the USA
Columbia, SC
04 October 2023